YORK NOTES

General Editors: Professor A.N. Jeffares (*University of Stirling*) & Professor Suheil Bushrui (*American University of Beirut*)

Jonathan Swift

GULLIVER'S TRAVELS

Notes by Richard Gravil

BA (WALES) PH D (EAST ANGLIA)
Reader in English Literature
University of Lodz, Poland

LONGMAN
YORK PRESS

YORK PRESS
Immeuble Esseily, Place Riad Solh, Beirut.

LONGMAN GROUP LIMITED
Longman House,
Burnt Mill,
Harlow,
Essex.

© Librairie du Liban 1980

First published 1980
Second impression 1985
ISBN 0 582 78165 5
Produced by Longman Group (FE) Ltd
Printed in Hong Kong

Contents

Part 1

Introduction

Life of Swift

Jonathan Swift was born on 30 November 1667 in Dublin. His father having died before Jonathan's birth, Swift was dependent on the family at large for his upbringing. He had four uncles to appeal to and it was the oldest, Godwin Swift, who saw to it that Jonathan received a good education, first at Kilkenny School and then at Trinity College, Dublin, from which he graduated in 1686. The family was an English one which had settled in Ireland shortly after the death of Swift's grandfather, Thomas Swift, a clergyman who had been removed from his church in Herefordshire during the Cromwellian period to be replaced by a Dissenting minister.

When political and civil strife broke out in Ireland after the Glorious Revolution of 1688 it was natural that Swift was among those who returned to England. At first he stayed with his mother in Leicester—though he had seen little of her during his childhood—but in 1689 family influence obtained for him the post of private secretary to Sir William Temple. Temple was a distinguished diplomat, now retired, a leading liberal, and a man of culture and intelligence. In his house, Moor Park in Surrey, Swift not only enjoyed a life of elegance and stimulating companionship, but became known to Temple's powerful friends in aristocratic and political circles.

Severe illness caused Swift to return to Ireland in the summer of 1690. He had experienced his first attack of Menière's disease—an illness which attacks the inner ear, causing giddiness, vomiting and deafness—which was to recur more violently in 1710 and with increasing intensity throughout his life. This disease was not medically recognised until 1861: its effects on a man of Swift's energies and temperament helped to create the legend of Swift the misanthrope and the madman, which it has taken a century of scholarship to dispel, especially as it seemed such a convenient explanation of the savage force of his satirical writings. In 1690, anyway, all his doctors could advise was a change of climate. But finding no work in Ireland he was soon back at Moor Park where he stayed from December 1691 to the summer of 1694. Here he developed his own literary powers, with access to Sir William's fine library, and found himself involved in political affairs. The environment fired his ambition too. While working on Temple's papers he was in reality waiting for King William to appoint him to a church living in England. In 1694, tired of waiting, and offended by the offer of an obscure appointment, he angered Temple by returning to Dublin. By the spring of 1695 he was installed in the parish of Kilroot, near Belfast.

But Kilroot could in no way compensate for Moor Park. By May 1696 he was back for his third stay with Temple. It was a wise move. Although when Temple died in 1699 Swift was still without a living, he had composed three of his most famous satires, *A Tale of a Tub, The Battle of the Books*, and the *Discourse Concerning the Mechanical Operation of the Spirit*.

Now thirty-two, Swift returned to Ireland as chaplain to the Earl of Berkeley, one of the Irish Lords Justice, and in the following year, 1700, became Vicar of Láracor, a parish north of Dublin in County Meath. Swift was certainly no less conscientious than the average churchman of the time but did not allow his work there to interrupt his political concerns. In 1701 he was in London again, with Berkeley, and wrote a pamphlet praising the conduct of the Whig, or liberal, leaders. In the guise of *A Discourse of the Contests and Dissensions between the Nobles and the Commons in Athens and Rome* this astute political service made his reputation. In the next few years that reputation leaped. He was soon known as the author of masterly pamphlets in the Whig interest as well as of *A Tale of a Tub* and *The Battle of the Books*, written at Moor Park but published only in 1704.

Despite a Royalist and High Church background Swift's intellectual upbringing had been thoroughly Whig, both in Temple's service and later in Berkeley's. The Whig party, which developed from moderately radical protestant groups in the late seventeenth-century parliament, was in the ascendancy, and its writers formed the intellectual establishment. In parliament the first minister, Sidney Godolphin (1645–1712), was himself a Tory, but served as Lord Treasurer of predominantly Whig governments from 1702 to 1710. During this period Swift formed friendships with members of the Godolphin ministry and with the writers Steele and Addison, and naturally he expected that the services he performed for the Whigs with his acid pen would be rewarded by promotion to an English bishopric. This was not merely cynical ambition. His loyalties were genuinely divided. In the years 1708–9 he was writing a series of deeply felt religious pamphlets, such as the *Sentiments of a Church of England Man* and the ironic *Argument against Abolishing Christianity*. While aiding the Whigs his deepest concern was the defence of Church interests, and by the end of the decade he found that the Whigs were likely to pass legislation damaging to the Church.

Eighteenth-century church legislation is pretty meaningless to us today, but two minor points must be explained here if we are to understand the dramatic political about-turn Swift was soon to make. He had been campaigning for a measure known as 'Remission of the First Fruits' to be extended to the Irish church (the 'first fruits' system meant that a new minister of the Church had to pay his first year's income to a superior, and it had been reformed in England but not in Ireland). The Whigs would only allow this as part of a deal including the repeal of the Test Act, which denied political office to non-Anglicans. In Swift's eyes this was too high a price to pay, for he feared the political tendencies of religious enthusiasts whether Catholic or Dissenters.

When the Whig ministry of Godolphin fell in 1710 Swift saw no reason to fall with them. The Tory leaders Harley and St John thought Swift's pen worth having on their side. Where Godolphin had tried to force a deal on Swift, the Tories in effect bought his services with the legislation he had worked for so long. Swift did his best to use his influence to help his old friends, the essayists Steele and Addison and the dramatist Congreve, but he soon found congenial friendships among the Tories. Dr Arbuthnot, the Queen's physician, was now a close friend, and Swift mixed with Harley and St John on terms which Godolphin had never permitted. He became one of the famous 'Scriblerus Club', an association of witty writers which included St John himself, Alexander Pope the famous poet, John Gay the dramatist, and Dr Arbuthnot.

As editor of a Tory journal, *The Examiner*, and author of a brilliant attack on Marlborough and the Whigs called *The Conduct of the Allies*, Swift helped to maintain public support for the Tory ministry. Yet once again his new friends were unable to obtain for him high office in the Church in England. Not even Harley could soften Queen Anne towards the author of *A Tale of a Tub* when her closest friends and advisers, the Duchess of Somerset and the Archbishop of York, had described that work as profane and irreligious. And in fairness to the Queen that criticism of Swift's religious polemic is hard to refute.

In 1714 instead of being appointed to a place in England he returned to Dublin as Dean of St Patrick's Cathedral. Disappointed though he was, the promotion had come just in time. The Tory ministry fell apart in dissensions. Swift visited London in a vain attempt to reconcile Harley and St John—by now known as the Earl of Oxford and Viscount Bolingbroke—but after the Queen's death in that year the Tories fell from power. A year later Bolingbroke was in exile in France, and Oxford was imprisoned in London, both under suspicion of treason. In Bolingbroke's case these suspicions were not groundless: he was welcome in France and on good terms with Jacobite sympathisers (those who wished to restore the Stuart dynasty with French aid). But Swift knew nothing against his friends and, though they had done little enough for him, he remained loyal to them when to do so was dangerous, even foolhardy. He defended them soberly in his *History of the Last Four Years of the Queen*: but this work of serious contemporary history was considered political dynamite and was not published until 1758. A different kind of defence, however, did appear in *Gulliver's Travels* (1726) in which his friends are combined in the giant form of Gulliver, tormented by Whiggish pygmies. This was published just three years after Bolingbroke's pardon and return from exile.

In Ireland Swift soon made new friends among the clergy, including Thomas Sheridan and Patrick Delaney. For the first few years his pen looked back, writing contemporary history in such works as the *Enquiry into the Behaviour of the Queen's Last Ministry*. But by 1720 he was deeply involved in Irish affairs. In that year the Whigs passed an act to increase the dependency of Ireland on Britain. In reply Swift wrote his *Proposal for the Universal Use of Irish Manufacture*, instructing his fellow-countrymen in the art of economic self-reliance. When the government of Sir Robert Walpole, the new Whig leader, sought to impose a new coinage on Ireland known as Wood's half-pence (because the Londoner William Wood had been granted a licence to mint the coins) Swift responded with his series of *Drapier's Letters*. These four brilliant pieces, under the pseudonym 'M.B. Drapier', culminated in *A Letter to the Whole People of Ireland* (1724) and succeeded in so uniting the Irish—at least the Anglo-Irish elite to which Swift belonged—that the project was dropped. A reward of £300 was offered for proof of the writer's identity but no one in Ireland would now convict Swift. He had become a national hero.

By this time he had started his great work, *Gulliver's Travels*, written in 1721–5. When he visited London to arrange publication in 1726 he met his old friends Pope, Arbuthnot and Bolingbroke. He even dined once with Walpole, whose ministry he had just been satirising in *Gulliver*. If Swift still thought of being able to make a career in England these last visits in 1726 and 1727 must have disillusioned him. The rest of his life was bound to Ireland where, despite himself, he had become a popular national figure. His later writings include the bitter *Short View of the State of Ireland* (1728) and his most brilliant short satire *A Modest Proposal* (1729). Throughout the thirties he was writing fine verse, including the autobiographical *Verses on the Death of Dr Swift* (1731), and in 1736 came a biting attack on the Irish Parliament, *The Legion Club*.

His illness had worsened steadily. In 1742 he was declared incapable of managing his own affairs, and he lingered on, in pain and isolation, until his death on 19 October 1745. He was buried in his own cathedral under an epitaph of his own composition, in Latin. We know it best in the version by another great Anglo-Irish writer, W.B. Yeats:

> *Swift has sailed into his rest;*
> *Savage indignation there*
> *Cannot lacerate his breast.*
> *Imitate him if you dare,*
> *World-besotted traveller; he*
> *Served human liberty.*

At his death it was found that Swift, who had in his lifetime given away perhaps a third of his modest income, had saved another third which he left for the building of a hospital for the insane. It was a characteristic parting stroke for one who had devoted his wit to exposing the infirmities of the world, and what the Scriblerans called its 'dulness', to protect from that world those whose wits had proved too infirm to take the strain of existence.

Varina, Stella and Vanessa

It is ironic that the name of this bachelor clergyman has always been associated, with much gossip and some fact, with three young women who entered his life at various critical points in his career.

At Kilroot, the remote parish where he worked in 1695, he proposed marriage to Jane Waring, whom he called 'Varina'. She rejected him at first and Swift's pride was stung. When in 1700 she changed her mind Swift had changed his. He offered marriage once more, but in such cold and insulting terms that he knew she could only reject them.

By then, in any case, Swift had played his part in the education of Esther Johnson, a girl in Temple's household at Moor Park. The connection was such that 'Stella', as he called her, decided to settle in Ireland after Swift's appointment at Laracor. With her companion Rebecca Dingley, Stella became Swift's life-long friend. Some people believe that they were secretly married. Swift and Stella were in daily contact when he was in Ireland, and he wrote to her and Rebecca an intimate journal throughout his visits to England—written in such intimate baby-talk at times that many readers find it embarrassing, but containing a brilliant picture of London society. Each year he celebrated her birthday in tender, playful verses. He seems to have deliberately kept his relationship with this brilliant younger woman at a playful level, perhaps fearful of its turning into a deeper passion. When she was sick Swift could scarcely bear it. When she died he could not bring himself to attend her funeral, but consoled himself by writing a moving account of her life: 'the truest, most virtuous, and valuable friend that I, or perhaps any other person, ever was blessed with'. The evil-minded like to speculate that Swift was haunted by the suspicion that he and Stella were blood-relations, illegitimate progeny of Sir William Temple and his father.

If there was a marriage between them it must have been as secret reassurance to Stella that another of Swift's suitors could never replace her. In London, during his visits on church business in 1707–9, and in the Tory period up to 1714, he had established a friendship with Esther Vanhomrigh, eldest daughter of a brilliant household which was a centre of Anglo-Irish society. 'Vanessa', as he called her, followed Swift to Ireland in 1714 driven by a passion which he could not return, though he had thoughtlessly encouraged her at the start, and which he fended off as gently as possible. The early part of this relationship is described in the poem 'Cadenus and Vanessa', where Cadenus (an anagram for *decanus*, Latin for Dean) subjects this unequal relationship to clear scrutiny at his expense more than hers. Vanessa died in 1723 after the affair had passed through many stormy episodes; it is well described in A.L. Rowse's *Jonathan Swift: Major Prophet* (1975).

Swift and the Church

The eighteenth century saw the rise of a sentimental view of man in which it was increasingly assumed that man is naturally good. It was the era of 'The Noble Savage'. Man's conduct is motivated, when social conditions are favourable, by sympathy and benevolence, and as he is naturally rational so he is naturally virtuous. Such ideas appear in the liberal philosophers of Swift's time, and again in William Godwin at the end of the century: they end up as utilitarianism in the Victorian period, and as liberal humanism today.

Swift was untouched by such ideas. He took a sternly traditional view of man as a fallen creature, in need of redemption, driven by lust, greed and envy, or almost anything but Reason. The attack on mankind in *Gulliver's Travels* may strike modern readers as too severe for a Christian writer, yet his critique is no more extreme than one might find in seventeenth-century sermons and a few years after Swift's death the great religious reformer John Wesley (1703–91) found in *Gulliver* admirable proofs for the doctrine of Original Sin.

Of course Wesley exhibits unmistakable religious zeal: what seems to be missing in Swift is any evidence of a joyful religious faith to offset his rigorous moral criticism. As an Anglican he seems to expend more energy mocking religious enthusiasm than encouraging faith. For this the reasons are historical. As we saw, his grandfather had been persecuted by evangelical Puritans in Cromwell's time. And in Ireland he belonged to a minority faith in a land of Catholics. To any Anglican Tory in Swift's day Dissent was considered synonymous with political tyranny, and Catholics were identified with Jacobite treason. Swift believed sincerely that the tolerant middle-of-the-road Anglican Church, associated with the kind of constitutional monarchy established by the Glorious Revolution of 1688, was the common-sense position. To defend religious liberty for all, it was paradoxically necessary to deny political power to Dissenters or to Catholics who, it was believed, would use such power to deny any liberty at all to people of other persuasions. To understand how natural it seemed in the age of Swift for a churchman to expend most of his energies in political activity it is necessary to look at the historical background, and the events to which *Gulliver's Travels* refers.

The Puritan Commonwealth

In 1629 King Charles I dissolved Parliament. Only when his attempt to impose his own religion on the Scots brought about a Scottish revolution did he summon Parliament again to raise money for an army. Parliament refused to subscribe, and in 1642 Charles fled from London and Parliament prepared for civil war: a war between 'Cavaliers' (Scots Catholics and English Royalists) on the one hand, and 'Roundheads' (Scots Presbyterians and English Protestants) on the other. In the course of the war Oliver Cromwell had trained a Roundhead army of exceptional effectiveness and religious zeal, which was unwilling to disband when Parliament attempted to dismiss it. A second civil war led to the execution of Charles in 1649, and the abolition of the Monarchy and of the House of Lords. For ten years England was ruled by Cromwell as Lord Protector, and by religious Dissenters, or Puritans. But the Commonwealth did not survive Cromwell's death.

The Restoration: Tories and Whigs

In 1660 Charles II was crowned, at the invitation of a newly elected Parliament. At first the transition was achieved peaceably. An Act of Indemnity prevented excessive acts of revenge, and a large body of former Roundheads remained in possession of lands and wealth formerly owned by Royalists. In consequence the Parliament of the early years was made up partly of old Cavaliers, the Tory squires, and partly of old Roundheads. The Tory majority began to exact a different kind of revenge by religious persecution of Dissenters. In the course of time the Roundhead element in Parliament began to gain strength, and the Tory or High Church Party found itself opposed by a Whig Party composed of Puritan sympathisers and progressive free-thinkers who believed in religious toleration, at least for Protestants.

The triple alliance

Unbelievably Charles II had learned little from his father's experience. Kept short of money by the Parliament which had restored his crown he looked increasingly towards France and alliance with Louis XIV. To most of his subjects, however, France was clearly the enemy—representing both 'Popery' (the English word for Catholicism) and tyranny. The people, and Parliament, were grateful to Sir William Temple whose diplomacy had allied England, the Netherlands and Sweden against the power of France in 1668. Charles, however, exploited the national feeling of commercial rivalry with Holland (there had been two Anglo-Dutch wars already) to undermine the alliance. He made a public treaty with Louis who wished to attack and partition Holland, and a private treaty that would enable him to use French money and French soldiers to support his plan to impose Catholicism and Absolute Monarchy on England. Only Holland's extraordinary victory put an end to this plot, and forced Charles to adapt himself to his Anglican Parliament. But Parliament, under Tory High Church dominance, used its new power to crush the Dissenters more vigorously than ever. In their turn the rising Whig party took savage revenge against suspected Catholics. The pendulum swung back and forth. And Parliament was again weakening itself by these factional feuds.

The Glorious Revolution of 1688

The first great event of James II's reign was a new Puritan revolt against the Catholic monarch, led by the Duke of Monmouth. Again the King's response was excessive. The flood of executions horrified moderate opinion, and James attempted to secure his power by recruiting an overwhelmingly Catholic army, which he installed near the capital to impress the people. He established a standing army of 30,000 men, and nothing could have alienated his natural supporters, the royalist Tory squires, more than this clumsy reminder of recent tyranny. James, in his policy of emulating Louis, antagonised both the English (including moderate Catholics) and the Pope himself. The English, watching the French persecution of the Huguenots (who arrived in England in thousands), saw that similar horrors were in store for them.

In 1688 William of Orange landed in Torbay. James's army deserted, and the people united about the new King William and his English Queen, Mary. The King was to rule with the consent of Parliament. Religious toleration became established, except that political power was denied to Catholics or Dissenters. A Protestant succession was assured. To most Englishmen, and certainly to Swift, the balance between King, Church, and Parliament, brought about by the so-called Revolution Settlement, was a triumph of common sense. It is certainly the foundation of Swift's political views.

War with France

The Revolution succeeded so painlessly because John Churchill, the future Duke of Marlborough, had abandoned James's army at the critical moment, and William's policy of containment of France was to be made possible by this brilliant soldier.

War with France was inevitable if William was to ensure the failure of Jacobitism, that is, attempts to restore James and a Catholic monarchy in Britain. Parliament willingly financed the campaign. Marlborough led Protestant Europe throughout the War of the Spanish Succession (1701–13) and won great victories at Blenheim in 1704, and Ramillies in 1706, while Prince Eugene of Savoy won similar victories in the South. Marlborough's conquests were achieved by military genius supported by an anti-Jacobite alliance of Whigs and moderate Tories, who controlled the parliamentary purse.

But war is expensive. By 1709 Louis and Marlborough, and most of the English people, were ready for a just peace. Except for occupation of France itself, war could accomplish no more. But the Whigs were after total victory, as war cabinets usually are. At this point a series of domestic disasters caused a change of government (and Swift's change of sides). Queen Anne had succeeded her brother-in-law in 1702: she, and her new Tory ministry of 1710, desired peace. In 1713 they achieved it by the controversial Treaty of Utrecht.

The treaty was deplored by the Whig leaders for its leniency to France, and when the Whigs returned to power in 1714 under the Hanoverian King George I both Oxford and Bolingbroke were impeached for their role in the secret negotiations that brought it about, negotiations that appeared the more treasonable since the Pretender (James III as he wished to be) was involved. The Whigs were to remain in power throughout the next two reigns, until 1760. For twenty-one of those years the country was governed by Sir Robert Walpole, who came to power in 1721, just as Swift was beginning Book 1 of *Gulliver's Travels* and looking at these events through the eyes of Gulliver.

The situation of Ireland

Ever since Pope Adrian IV requested King Henry II to conquer Ireland in 1154 there had been Norman, English or Scottish elements in possession of parts of Ireland. But no monarch ever succeeded in making a real union between the Irish and the other British peoples. About once a century the Irish revolted and were put down by the English, some of whom remained to be absorbed by the Irish and participate in the next rising. The major result of this policy of alternate neglect and punitive raids was that Ireland remained a poor country whose native people were almost wholly Catholic and sympathetic to a whole succession of enemies of England—from Spain in Elizabeth's time to the French in Swift's.

Swift thought of himself as English. At the time of the Battle of the Boyne, when William defeated James II in 1690 (the Glorious Revolution had been peaceful in England but was bloody in Ireland), Swift was with Temple in Surrey. Yet from 1714 onwards he became increasingly known as an Irish patriot. What he experienced in Ireland was very similar to the experience of the American colonists under George III—all the disadvantages of direct rule from London, and none of the advantages. Since no politician in England gave much thought to Ireland the land was bled by absentee landlords, denied fair trading terms, and ruled by second-rate officials who could behave irresponsibly with no one to care about the consequences. Hardly any of the major posts in Irish administration were filled by native-born Irishmen.

In the face of neglect, decay and outright oppression, Swift became a reluctant patriot, showing how the colonial power might be resisted. There was nothing radical about Swift's social and political views. He believed in order and authority—though less so when authority was Whig. He believed that society is a hierarchy in which Princes owe protection to their subjects, and masters to their servants, while these in turn owe loyalty to their masters and princes. What was radical was that he applied this belief to Ireland. The Anglo-Irish, he felt, had been denied their rights as free men. The Irish were oppressed because they were not enjoying the fair application of the principles of the Revolution Settlement. He felt he was living among a nation of 'beggars, thieves, oppressors, fools and knaves', but scornful though he was towards the Irish and their unwillingness to help themselves, his most savage indignation was reserved for Ireland's absentee government. Walpole's Whig ministry in London was the real target of a stream of pamphlets he produced on Irish matters in the 1720s, the decade of *Gulliver's Travels*.

Some of Swift's other works

It was *A Tale of a Tub*, written mostly in 1696 and published anonymously in 1704, that made Swift's literary reputation. It makes difficult reading today because it is written in a skilful parody of learned ecclesiastical English. This was the work which offended Queen Anne, and many other readers, since it is easy to see it as a mockery of all religious belief. It was intended as a fable demonstrating that of all the varieties of Christianity available in the eighteenth century the Anglican is the purest, or at least relatively free of corruptions.

The Battle of the Books, published with the *Tale*, is Swift's contribution to a debate started by Sir William Temple as to whether ancient or modern writings were of greater value. In its argument that modern thinkers are guilty of pride in neglecting the wisdom of the past the *Battle*, though written in an allusive and learned style, is closely related to two sections of Gulliver's third voyage, the attack on modern science in Laputa, and Gulliver's talks with the spirits in Glubbdubdrib.

The first pamphlet Swift wrote in defence of the Whigs was his *Discourse of the Contests and Dissensions in Athens and Rome* (1701). To an Irishman, only two years after William had defeated the Jacobite forces in Ireland, the rising power of the Tories and their willingness to go to extreme lengths to discredit the Whigs were very alarming matters. *The Contests and Dissensions* is a warning to the Tories not to weaken the nation by their partisan activities—though Swift also cautions the Whigs against giving encouragement to Dissenters.

The *Argument against Abolishing Christianity* (1708) is one of a number of religious works written at the time Swift was becoming uneasy about the Whigs. More important, it is also one of his most exuberantly ironical pieces, the first to be written in Swift's wonderful combination of plain English with elaborate flights of irony.

The finest of Swift's achievements as a Tory propagandist was his *The Conduct of the Allies* (1711), which helped to bring about peace by describing the war with France as a national calamity continued for private profit by Marlborough and Godolphin. Fair or not, the pamphlet is persuasive and hard hitting, and provided the Tories with most of their arguments in parliamentary debate. It finished Marlborough's career.

Swift's first influential contribution to Irish affairs was *A Proposal for the Universal Use of Irish Manufacture* (1720). Trading arrangements appeared to be fixed with a view to the deliberate ruination of Ireland. Here Swift asserts the right of the Irish to import and export as their own needs required, rather than under legislation designed to protect England's trade at Ireland's expense.

His most savage work, *A Modest Proposal* (1729), was again inspired by the sufferings of Ireland. In matter-of-fact style such as any economist might have used, Swift argues that the twin problems of famine and overpopulation could be solved simultaneously by feeding the children of the poor to the households of the rich. The landlords having 'already devoured most of the parents, seem to have the best title to the children'. By breeding especially for the meat market Ireland could also increase its exports, and Swift skilfully turns the screw of horror with each new phase of his argument. In a final hit at Whig indifference to Irish sufferings he suggests that an added advantage of his proposal is that it runs no danger of 'disobliging England'.

Of some hundred works of verse, satire, parody, history, polemic, and devotion, these titles perhaps give an indication of the course of Swift's career. *Gulliver's Travels* is the work of a man who could excel at the clear and persuasive sermon, the most scurrilous political lampoon, solid history, or baroque exercises of fancy.

A note on the text

Some parts of the first two voyages may have been written as early as 1714, when Swift was in London and the Scriblerus Club planned to collaborate on a work called 'The Memoirs of Martinus Scriblerus', to include four journeys such as Gulliver undertakes. But Swift began in earnest in 1721, finishing Books 1 and 2 in the following year, writing Book 4 in 1723, and book 3 in 1724–5 (while also engaged with the *Drapier's Letters*). In 1725 he revised the whole work and it was published on 28 October 1726 by Benjamin Motte who had received the manuscript only two months before, and as Pope reported, 'he knew not from whence, nor from whom, dropped at his house in the dark, from a hackney coach'. Although Swift knew that publishing satire was a risky business he was angered by the first edition, in which the printer had made a number of alterations and omissions. Charles Ford, a friend who had arranged the original publication to preserve Swift's anonymity, made a list of corrections which were printed in the revised edition of 1727. The 'Letter from Captain Gulliver to his Cousin Sympson' which opens the book is dated 2 April 1727 and was written for this edition, which was in fact the fourth, since three editions had sold out in the first year. But this edition was still not as Swift wanted it. The first edition to include all the corrections Swift wanted was published by Faulkner in Dublin in 1735. All modern editions now follow this text, including passages which Motte had not dared to print. In these notes quotations are taken from a modernised spelling edition, the Signet Classic, New American Library, New York, 1960.

Part 2

Summaries
of GULLIVER'S TRAVELS

A general summary

In appearance *Gulliver's Travels* is the sole work of Captain Lemuel Gulliver, an educated seafaring man who has set down his memoirs of four voyages to remote countries of the world as a contribution to human knowledge. In reality it is the masterpiece of Jonathan Swift: an elaborate concoction of political allegory, moral fable, social anatomy, and mock Utopias, set within a skilful parody of both travel fiction and journals of scientific exploration.

In his first voyage, to Lilliput, Gulliver is shipwrecked on an unknown island near Sumatra and wakes to find himself the captive of a race of people six inches tall. As he describes the history and customs of these people they seem remarkably similar, at times, to the English. In the satirical pattern of the work, Book 1 presents a detailed political allegory of the reigns of Queen Anne and George I of England. Not for a moment does Gulliver cease to be Gulliver, yet his services to the state and his near impeachment for treason bear a curious resemblance to the experiences of the Earl of Oxford and Viscount Bolingbroke.

In Book 2, Gulliver is accidentally abandoned by his shipmates in an unmapped region of North America where the inhabitants are twelve times his size. Here Gulliver is adopted as a pet, and exhibited as a freak of nature. Both scale and plot are reversed. Brobdingnag, unlike Lilliput, bears little resemblance to England, but the political theme is continued with Gulliver as a representative eighteenth-century Englishman attempting to justify the human race under the gentle interrogation of a benevolent giant king.

Book 3 opens with Gulliver captured by pirates and abandoned to his fate near some small islands in the vicinity of Japan. He is taken aboard the flying island of Laputa, inhabited by people who are obsessed by abstract sciences and speculations, yet are able, by their superior position, to tyrannise the land of Balnibarbi beneath them. That we are back in the ill-governed Britain of George I is soon apparent, for Book 3 is full of contemporary detail. But the satire is less political than intellectual, examining man's claims to be a rational creature by showing us numerous examples of how man abuses his reasoning powers, and how absurd, irrelevant, and dangerously irresponsible an intelligentsia can be. From Balnibarbi Gulliver makes an excursion to Glubbdubdrib, the island of Sorcerers, where his host allows him to hold conversations with the moral giants of ancient history, the 'immortals' of our culture. But if he is under any illusion that real immortality would improve humankind his next excursion, to Luggnagg, disillusions him. Here he meets the race of Struldbrugs, fated to everlasting senility, the most mortifying sight he ever beheld.

Book 4 completes the satirical argument by creating a Utopia of pure reason and measuring man against this impossible standard. On his first voyage as Captain he is the victim of a mutiny. Abandoned on shore he encounters a noble race of horses, the Houyhnhnms, and their 'cattle', the Yahoos. Despite their human shape Gulliver finds the Yahoos the most 'disagreeable animal' he had encountered in all his travels. By contrast the Houyhnhnms appear to be 'the perfection of nature' and Gulliver comes to love their way of life. The grace and dignity of the philosopher-horses is all the more effective for being preceded in the travels by a succession of humanoid races, the absurd and spiteful Lilliputians, the grotesque Brobdingnagians, and the intellectual freaks of Book 3. But the Houyhnhnms regard Gulliver as a kind of Yahoo, a view which he is forced to share. Exiled from the land of these 'inimitable' beings, Gulliver returns unwillingly to England, where he divides his time between talking to his horses and attempting to 'reform the Yahoo race in this kingdom'.

So Gulliver, it appears in retrospect, is not simply the amiable companion we first took him for. He is a man who has seen a vision of perfection: a man with a mission. That mission is to prepare us step by step to recognise ourselves, in the final book, as 'Yahoos in shape and disposition'.

Detailed summaries

A letter from Captain Gulliver to his Cousin Sympson

In this opening letter, first added to the second edition, Captain Gulliver complains on Swift's behalf about changes made by the printer in the first edition, some of them real, and some imaginary. The fact that Swift here continues the fiction that the work is by Gulliver is not the only joke in the letter. For Swift sustains the characterisation of the Captain as he appeared at the end of Book 4. In a tone of moral indignation Gulliver professes his inability to lie or to deceive, yet all the time he is referring solemnly to imaginary places and beings, and providing clues to Swift's satirical design. For instance he names two of Swift's literary sources, first by claiming to be a cousin of Dampier, on whose *Voyage round the World* the travels are closely modelled, and later by rejecting the slanders that his work is fictional, or that it bears any relation to *Utopia*.

The letter is an excellent introduction to Swift's ironic method and to his use of the character of Gulliver. His most innocent disclaimers often turn out to be the most directly satirical strokes. For instance, disclaiming any lack of respect for Queen Anne he thereby introduces her name and those of her ministers Godolphin and Oxford into the first page of the book. He professes not to understand the word 'innuendo', and then explicitly links 'people in power' to 'the Yahoos who are now said to govern the herd'. Gulliver contradicts himself almost from one line to the next. His list of the 'reformations' he expected to see as a consequence of publishing his book is of course a summary of the criticisms of society made throughout the *Travels*. Yet in the next sentence he confesses to a conviction that Yahoos are not really 'capable of the least disposition to virtue or wisdom' so are presumably incapable of reformation. Then he complains indignantly that readers have accused him of criticising statesmen, degrading human nature, and abusing the female sex—which is a pretty fair summary of what the book does throughout. What are we to make of it all? On the one hand Swift is clearly making fun of his misanthropic sailor. On the other hand Gulliver, who does not exist, can hardly be held responsible for the satirical content of the work. So where does Swift really stand? To that question every reader must find his own answer.

NOTES AND GLOSSARY:

Dampier: Sir William Dampier (1652–1715) published his vivid narrative of *A New Voyage round the World* in 1697

Utopia: Sir Thomas More (1478–1535) published his *Utopia*, an account of an imaginary island with an ideal political system, in 1514

The Publisher to the Reader

In his prefatory note the imaginary Richard Sympson offers a short and pedantic account of Lemuel Gulliver. He admits to 'some relation between us by the mother's side' without going so far as to say 'cousin Gulliver'. Clearly this family of Gullivers and Sympsons is of a cautious disposition. Sympson claims to have removed from the text 'innumerable passages' of nautical pedantry to make the work more readable.

A Voyage to Lilliput: Chapter 1

Gulliver begins with a short autobiography, to acquaint us with his background and professional experience. By the fourth paragraph he has set sail from Bristol for a voyage to the South Seas. His ship, the *Antelope*, is wrecked on 5 November 1699 and Gulliver loses his companions when their lifeboat is overturned. He swims and wades ashore and, finding no inhabitants, falls asleep. When he wakes he finds that he cannot move: even his hair is tied to the ground. Something is creeping up his left leg, and when it reaches his chin he sees 'a human creature not six inches high'. Attempting to free himself he is pierced by tiny arrows and decides not to resist. A 'person of quality' makes a long speech 'whereof I understood not one syllable', but he is fed on baskets of meat and barrels of wine. Feeling in debt to such hospitality, and drugged by wine, Gulliver relapses into sleep while the Lilliputians convey him ingeniously to their capital city. 'Fifteen hundred of the Emperor's largest horses, each about four inches and a half high' are employed for the half-mile journey which takes a day and a half. On arrival Gulliver is lodged in the nation's largest temple, into which he can just creep: secured by ninety-one watch-chains 'locked to my left leg with six and thirty padlocks'. Even in this chapter of eventful narrative, notice the play of Swift's irony. Gulliver has, on wakening, accepted his powerlessness in the hands of the Lilliputian state, and uses the most courteous titles in reference to his captors. He has begun also to note the language, and to observe the excellence of their science: so excellent, Gulliver claims, with unconscious irony, that they were able to raise him three inches in less than three hours!

NOTES AND GLOSSARY:

Van Diemen's Land: modern Tasmania

Chapter 2

Gulliver's delight in his new surroundings is reflected in Swift's entertaining description of events and objects. But many of these effects are already ironical, especially when Gulliver refers to the 'majestic' deportment of the Emperor, whom he has to observe by lying down, and who supposes that he can defend himself with his three-inch sword. Similarly, Gulliver's pleasure in having his mercy to six ruffians well received at court, the corruption of secretaries of state, who sell licences to people who wish to view the 'Man-Mountain', and the manner in which Gulliver is searched by security officers, whom he has to put in each pocket in turn, are none the less satirical for Gulliver's solemn style of narration. An inventory of his possessions is made, in which common items, such as his snuff-box and comb, are described as they would be by somebody wholly ignorant of their purposes. This stylistic device combines surprise and pleasure with the important effect of establishing the foreignness of Gulliver.

NOTES AND GLOSSARY:

The Emperor: with his 'Austrian lip', the Emperor is a satirical portrait of the Hanoverian King George I, who was anything but 'graceful' or 'well-proportioned' in unflattering eyes

High and Low Dutch: German and Dutch

The Inventory: this may suggest the similarly minute investigation made by the Whigs into the affairs of the fallen Tory leaders, Oxford and Bolingbroke, in 1715. Swift viewed Oxford especially as a giant among pygmies

My pocket perspective: a pocket telescope

Chapter 3

An innocent opening paragraph leads directly into a chapter of court satire. The practice of selecting candidates for high office by their skill in walking the tight-rope, or of awarding decorations to the most accomplished creepers, is clearly meant to typify the court of George I, or indeed any government. Gulliver entertains and impresses the court himself, by assisting at military parades and exercises. He then obtains his 'liberty' by consenting to a series of conditions devised by the Admiral of the Realm, beginning with an amusing form of address to the Emperor (not without some resemblance to styles of address used by some potentates today) and containing eight clauses. The seventh in effect sentences Gulliver to hard labour in his leisure hours, and it is worth examining the other seven for their combination of prudence, oddity and malignancy. Gulliver appears to be impressed by his allowance of food sufficient for the support of 1728 Lilliputians (and by their ability to calculate 12^3) but his reference to 'the prudent and exact economy of so great a prince' is not without irony, any more than his sense that he is now 'at full liberty'.

NOTES AND GLOSSARY:

Flimnap: the agile Flimnap is generally agreed to be a portrait of Sir Robert Walpole, and the 'cushion' which

saves Flimnap's neck may be a reference to one of
the King's mistresses, the Duchess of Kendal, who
helped to restore Walpole to office in 1721. Walpole
was first minister in 1715–17 and again from 1721
to 1742. For identification of other characters see
Part 3 of these notes

Chapter 4

A description of the capital and the Emperor's palace is followed by an
interview with Reldresal, Principal Secretary of Private Affairs (itself
a satirical title), who outlines the political problems of the Empire.
There are two factions, the High-Heels and Low-Heels, of which the
former is larger and more traditional, but the latter, favoured by the
Emperor, is in power. This division corresponds to the High and Low
Church parties of Swift's day, the Tories and Whigs, in which George
I favoured the latter but the Crown Prince kept in with both parties,
that is, 'hobbled' with one heel higher than the other. A greater problem
is that of the Big-Endian faction. The Big-Endians (who, like Catholics
in England, were prevented from holding certain offices) were in league
with the rival empire of Blefuscu against Lilliput's Little-Endian
dynasty. The two states had been at war for years, and Lilliput,
Reldresal confides, stood in fear of invasion by the new Blefuscudian
war fleet.

NOTES AND GLOSSARY:

Historical allusions: For fuller interpretation of this chapter see the
historical introduction and the discussion of Swift's
political allegory in Part 3. The 'bloody war' is the
War of the Spanish Succession' (1701–13). 'His
present Majesty's grandfather' is a loose reference
to Henry VIII and the English Reformation. 'One
Emperor lost his life, and another his crown':
Charles I, executed in 1649, and James II, deposed
in 1688

Chapter 5

Taking Reldresal's hint, Gulliver wades across the channel between
Lilliput and Blefuscu and captures fifty men-of-war which he tows back
to Lilliput. For this feat he is created a Nardac (a Duke) but his
reluctance to aid the Emperor in his plans to subjugate Blefuscu
completely, though supported by 'the wiser part of the ministry', soon

brings him into disfavour. Gulliver's disillusion appears in his remark: 'Of so little weight are the greatest services to princes, when put into the balance with a refusal to gratify their passions'. A favourable treaty is arranged but his friendly relations with ambassadors from Blefuscu make matters still worse. In a second exploit Gulliver offends the Empress. He saves her palace from burning down by 'voiding' his urine 'in such a quantity ... that in three minutes the fire was wholly extinguished'.

NOTES AND GLOSSARY:

The Palace fire: In one interpretation of this incident Gulliver represents Swift himself, the 'conflagration' suggests fires of religious enthusiasm, the 'noble pile, which had cost so many ages in erecting' is the Church of England, and the device by which the flames are extinguished is Swift's *A Tale of a Tub*, which so offended Queen Anne. But the story also fits the Treaty of Utrecht, in which, by secret negotiations with the enemy, Oxford and Bolingbroke had used illegal means to extinguish a conflagration

Chapter 6

This detailed account of Lilliputian customs and institutions is to be read warily. Although the nastiness of the Lilliputians is clear enough in Chapters 4 and 5 there is no guarantee that the same point of view will remain. After a playful comparison of the Lilliputian way of writing with that of ladies in England, Gulliver explains their burial rites, which he finds absurd, and passes on to other peculiar customs. These include punishing defrauders and false informers, rewarding merit, giving office to the virtuous rather than the intelligent, disqualifying atheists from office, executing the ungrateful, educating children in state nurseries (and allowing their parents to see them twice a year), and too many other points to list. Gulliver describes his domestic and tailoring arrangements, and a visit from the Emperor and other court notables, and finally defends himself with some heat from the accusation of having had an affair with the Treasurer's wife, perhaps one of the least probable flirtations in imaginative literature.

NOTES AND GLOSSARY:

Flimnap's white staff: a white staff was the symbol of office of the English Lord Treasurer

Lilliputian customs: Swift's attitude to the employment of atheists, or the education of working-class children, would not be that of a modern liberal, though he would certainly have liked begging to be 'a trade unknown in this kingdom'. Each point in this sometimes Utopian account of Lilliput should be weighed with care, not just to detect what Swift might have thought, for he intends his reader to enjoy sifting the passage for its sense and nonsense, and the tone makes it as hard as possible to distinguish between them

Chapter 7

In tones of deep political intrigue Gulliver reveals how he was made aware of a plot to impeach him for treason. The articles of impeachment (in which Swift is satirising similar charges made against his friends) accuse him of 'maliciously' putting out a fire 'under colour of extinguishing' a fire, and of conversing with ambassadors, whose business it is to converse, and of treacherously planning a journey to Blefuscu with *only* his Imperial Majesty's permission. In a classic parody of the reasonable arguments politicians (or people) can always find for the most despicable actions, Gulliver's informant explains how the court plans to take his life. He is to be blinded, assuming he will lie down for the operation: 'It would be sufficient for you to see by the eyes of the ministers, since the greatest princes do no more'. Then he will be starved, by degrees, until his corpse is lean enough to cause the least threat to public health. His sceptical reference to the Emperor's 'lenity and tenderness' is one ironical note in Gulliver's response, but you will detect others. Notice how Swift manages to suggest that Gulliver's sense of indebtedness might make him compliant, and that in reality the sentence was indeed a relatively mild one. Many political victims of our century might agree. But Gulliver takes advantage of 'his Imperial Majesty's licence' to visit Blefuscu, and having dutifully notified the Secretary, wades across the channel where he enjoys a reception 'suitable to the generosity of so great a prince'.

Chapter 8

In Blefuscu Gulliver notices a 'real boat' off shore, and with the aid of twenty Blefuscudian war-ships he beaches it. A demand arrives from Lilliput that Gulliver be sent back to them 'bound hand and foot'. The

Blefuscudian Emperor reasonably declares this to be impossible, and sends the good news of Gulliver's impending departure, while secretly asking our hero to remain in his service. Nonchalantly Gulliver remarks that he had a mind to take home 'a dozen of the natives' as a souvenir, but that his Majesty engaged his honour not to do so, besides diligently searching his pockets. He sets sail, recording his nautical progress as usual, and is soon picked up by an English merchant vessel, whose friendly captain finds Gulliver's story a little on the tall side. Six months later he arrives home, little changed by his experiences. He sets out again only two months later, having provided for his family. In a final joke at Gulliver's expense Swift has him speculate on his plans to breed Lilliputian sheep for the wool trade, perhaps a foretaste of the Academy of Projectors in Book 3.

A Voyage to Brobdingnag: Chapter 1

With Captain Nicholas of Cornwall, Gulliver sets sail for Surat in *The Adventure*. After wintering at the Cape of Good Hope they run into foul weather and are blown five hundred leagues off course. Land is sighted on 16 June 1703, and Gulliver, ashore in search of water, is abandoned by his shipmates who are chased off by a 'monster'. Gulliver too runs away, until he finds himself in a cornfield being harvested by people as tall as church steeples. Knowing that human creatures are 'more savage and cruel in proportion to their bulk' (Gulliver seems blessed with a very short memory) he expects to be eaten by these 'barbarians'. His finder, however, treats him as one would 'a small dangerous animal', and Gulliver begins to ingratiate himself with his captors by a display of humility and good manners. Taken home by a farmer he describes his first experience of life in a giant family, with baby, cat, dogs and rats all of terrifying proportions. He is almost swallowed by a year-old child, and is horrified at the sight of the baby feeding from a 'monstrous' nipple. He slays a rat with his sword, and as in the first chapter of Book 1, gives a circumstantial account of his first experience of discharging 'the necessities of nature'. Mathematicians may like to calculate how much less of a problem this would be than it was in Lilliput, though if anything, Gulliver's embarrassment is increased. Physicality is clearly going to be a major theme of this book.

Chapter 2

Gulliver is practically adopted by Glumdalclitch, the nine-year-old daughter of the house: 'she was very good natured, and not above forty foot high, being little for her age'. She calls him 'Grildrig' or mannikin. News of his arrival spreads, and Gulliver's 'master', as he already calls him, decides to make a quick fortune by exhibiting this entertaining freak. He is carried about in a box and shown at the nearest market town with such success that they set out on a two-month tour of towns and country houses on the way to the capital, Lorbrulgrud, or 'Pride of the Universe'. Meanwhile Glumdalclitch teaches him the language.

Chapter 3

Too frequent shows begin to damage Gulliver's health, but after an appearance at court Gulliver is bought by the Queen who also takes Glumdalclitch into her service. He makes a flattering speech in the language of Brobdingnag, which the Queen takes as proof of his 'wit and sense'. The King at first takes him for a 'splacknuck', as does everyone else (Gulliver has already assured us that a splacknuck, though a small animal, is 'very finely shaped'). Next he is taken for a clockwork toy. The court scholars, like those of Lilliput, do not really believe in his existence and finally pronounce him a *lusus naturae* (Latin for a freak of nature). A cabinet-maker produces a wooden house for him, 'like a London bed-chamber' says Gulliver, though resembling a doll's-house. Gulliver dines with the Queen, another nauseous experience, and talks with the King about 'the manners, religion, laws, government and learning of Europe' to the great merriment of the King who 'observed how contemptible a thing was human grandeur which could be mimicked by such diminutive insects as I'. While Gulliver writhes in embarrassment, Swift puts into the King's mouth his own views of human society which is now seen clearly as Lilliputian. Gulliver also begins to see something of his own absurdity, at least physically, as he suffers indignities at the hands of the Queen's dwarf and fights off flies and wasps the size of larks and partridges.

NOTES AND GLOSSARY:
The Royal Sovereign: a large British warship built in 1637
Gresham College: a science institute which housed the Royal Society until 1666

Chapter 4

The country is described. Although the size of North America it does not appear on any maps, and it has no ports: since whales are the only sea-food large enough to eat there is no fishing industry. The account of the capital is notable for Gulliver's description of its beggars with their cancers and lice. A travelling closet is made for Gulliver, but he is not an impressionable tourist and is disappointed by the tower of the nation's chief temple: 'the height is not above three thousand foot'. For some reason he is more impressed by finding a 'little finger' four feet long fallen from a statue, and by the king's oven, though it is 'not so wide ... as the cupola of St Paul's'. These details are not accidental. It is only natural that Gulliver should be most interested in things whose size is within his grasp: and Swift is concerned with the horror of human realities more than with the grandeur of human impossibilities.

NOTES AND GLOSSARY:

St Paul's: The City of London's famous cathedral, designed by Sir Christopher Wren (1632–1723), was finished in 1716, replacing an earlier cathedral which had been severely damaged in the Great Fire of London, 1666. The central dome reaches 365 feet

Chapter 5

The dwarf repays a foolish pun by showering Gulliver with dwarf apples the size of barrels, and Gulliver suffers other calamities. He is picked up by a spaniel, falls into a mole-hill, does battle with a linnet (a small song-bird), and jumps into a fresh heap of cow-dung. Hit by hailstones he finds it necessary to 'weigh and measure' them in order to discover that they are 'near eighteen hundred times as large as those in Europe' (is this a comment on Gulliver's pedantry, or that of scientists in general?). But three episodes in the chapter are of deeper significance. Gulliver's experiences in the hands and bosoms of the Maids of Honour allow Swift one of his most wicked assaults on court morals, and while he is accusing them of sexual licence, and perhaps indulging in a little sexual fantasy, he slips in a mathematically calculated insult on the subject of smell: 'I cannot forbear doing justice to the Queen ... and Glumdalclitch, whose persons were as sweet as those of any lady in England'. The description which follows, of the execution of a murderer, is robbed of none of its force by Gulliver's calm description. But the longest episode in the chapter shows Gulliver kidnapped by a monkey who attempts to suckle him like an infant. That the monkey is the only creature in Brobdingnag who really regards Gulliver as one of his own species is one of Swift's most calculated shocks to the complacency of his reader (but remember that Darwin's *The Descent of Man* was not published until 1871). Gulliver's attempts to regain his, and our, dignity, are greeted with mockery by the court.

Chapter 6

Gulliver amuses himself making a comb out of hairs from the king's beard, and attempting to play the spinet (a small harpsichord), but this amusing opening is the prelude to Swift's sharpest satire in the second voyage. Wishing for 'the tongue of Demosthenes or Cicero' Gulliver attempts to impress the King with a description of his 'own dear native country'. He clearly does this very eloquently, in terms very far from those Swift would use, but the King proposes a number of innocent but searching questions, to each of which it would be härd to give an answer at once honest and encouraging. He is clearly an expert cross-examiner, or rather Swift is adept at mounting a satirical attack by nothing more than a series of rhetorical questions. Of course Gulliver's speech is ironical in itself. The cross-examination merely sharpens the attack, however gently done. But in the final paragraph, after a careful review of all the evidence, the King delivers to 'my little friend Grildrig' a devastating judgement: 'I cannot but conclude the bulk of your natives to be the most pernicious race of little odious vermin that nature ever suffered to crawl upon the surface of the earth'. The ironic and rhetorical arrangement of this whole chapter is worth the closest study, with its slow and logical build-up, the deceptively amicable setting, and the measured and unanswerable final sentence.

NOTES AND GLOSSARY:

Demosthenes: a great Athenian orator, Demosthenes (*c.* 383–322 BC) was a noble but somewhat humourless character. A master of words and argument, he rarely flattered his audience

Cicero: Marcus Tullius Cicero (106–43BC) was consul of Rome in 63 BC. Murdered by the second triumvirate, Antony, Octavian, and Lepidus, after the assassination of Caesar, he was an unbending idealist who developed a clear and fluent style in his many writings on law, government and moral philosophy

Generals richer than our Kings: a reference to the Duke of Marlborough, enriched by years of soldiering

Chapter 7

The ironic attack on human folly, duplicity and depravity which has been raised to such a pitch in the previous chapter is now sustained, for the first time, without relief, but by a variety of means. First Gulliver confesses that the King's verdict is based on partial evidence, for 'I artfully eluded many of his questions'. Then he attempts to explain the King's reaction as the effect of 'a certain narrowness of thinking' (narrow as opposed to lax?). And next he attempts to please the King by offering him the secret of gunpowder, which he commends by a catalogue of the ways which civilised nations have devised to destroy as many of each other as possible. The King is horrified by this brisk account and protests that he 'would rather lose half his kingdom than be privy to such a secret'. How strange, Gulliver thinks (and his thought seems to express the real political instinct of man, rather than the ideals we profess), 'that a prince ... should from a nice unnecessary scruple, whereof we in Europe can have no conception, let slip an opportunity put into his hands, that would have made him absolute master of the lives, the liberties, and the fortunes of his people'. But this King is a poor political philosopher, ignorant of 'mystery, refinement and intrigue'. In the remainder of the chapter the Utopian element of Brobdingnag becomes apparent. It is a land of useful science, simple laws, and good agriculture. Apart from a work of moral philosophy which looks back to an age when men must have been much larger, since they are now so physically frail, their books are few and profound. Gulliver approves of their prose style, in a verdict on Swift's own. A well-disciplined army is described, and Gulliver wonders why Brobdingnag needs an army at all. He is told that even in Brobdingnag there used to be wars, 'the nobility often contending for power, the people for liberty, and the King for absolute dominion', but that two reigns ago a 'general composition' was agreed by all three parties, since when the 'militia' have been kept under firm restrictions.

NOTES AND GLOSSARY:

General composition: clearly represents the Revolution Settlement which was the basis of Swift's political views. But Brobdingnag has evidently learned how to do without standing armies; England, Swift implies, has not

---

Chapter 8

The King begins to think of breeding more creatures like Gulliver (he is clearly beginning to be corrupted, as Gulliver was in Lilliput) but the latter is returned to liberty by the aid of a passing eagle who flies off with his box and drops it into the sea. Still inside his box Gulliver wonders why the captain of a passing ship does not order one of his sailors to 'put his finger into the ring' and lift the box on board. His rescuer, Captain Willcocks of Shropshire, treats Gulliver kindly, but is troubled by his apparent insanity until the whole story has been told, and some of Gulliver's remarkable souvenirs produced in evidence. The size of everything on the ship provokes Gulliver to laughter, and he explains that he had accustomed himself to life in Brobdingnag where 'I winked at my own littleness as people do at their own faults'. Nine months later he has still not come to terms with his real stature, as his comical homecoming shows.

NOTES AND GLOSSARY:

Places: Among the place-names in this chapter, Tonquin is Tongking, Vietnam; New Holland is Australia

---

A Voyage to Laputa, Balnibarbi, Glubbdubdrib, Luggnagg, and Japan: Chapter 1

Gulliver is persuaded by Captain William Robinson to be surgeon on the *Hopewell* for a voyage to the East Indies, and they set sail in August 1706, via Fort St George (Madras). To pass the time during delays at Tonquin, Gulliver takes command of a sloop—a small single-masted vessel—which is first caught in a storm and then boarded by pirates, who include a Japanese captain and a Dutch sailor. Gulliver's men are taken prisoner, while he himself is 'set adrift in a small canoe' thanks to the Japanese who obstructs the Dutchman's more hostile intentions. He makes his way to some distant islands which appear uninhabited. Walking in the heat of the day he is surprised to find the sun suddenly obscured by 'a vast opaque body', a flying island. He attracts the attention of these airborne islanders, first by shouting and then with his usual 'supplicating postures', and is lifted into the island.

NOTES AND GLOSSARY:

Japan: foreign trade with Japan was monopolised throughout the sixteenth to eighteenth centuries first by Portugal and then by Holland, with occasional English intrusions. Whichever nation was in favour at the time did its best to exclude the others. Hence the conduct of the Dutch sailor in this chapter, and Gulliver's behaviour in Chapter 11

Chapter 2

Swift's satire on intellectual absurdities opens with a description of the islanders. The people of 'quality', that is, the ruling class, are perpetually lost in deep speculation, their heads inclined to left or right, 'one of their eyes turned inward, and the other directly up to the zenith'. Their clothes are decorated with astronomical and musical motifs. They are attended by 'flappers' whose task is to remind their absent-minded masters that they were about to speak, or are being spoken to, or are in danger of collision, by gently flapping their mouth, ears or eyes, with a kind of rattle. Gulliver is introduced to the king, and gives the court 'a very mean opinion of my understanding' by refusing the aid of a flapper. He eats a meal, each item cut into mathematical or musical figures, and sets about learning the language, especially of course its astronomical, geometrical and musical terms, while Swift slips in a parody of improbable etymology in Gulliver's speculation on the origin of the word 'Laputa'. He is measured for a suit of clothes, with ill-fitting results, and discovers that their houses are ill-built for the same reason: his hosts being interested only in theoretical mathematics, they have a contempt for practical geometry. That this does not discourage passionate political disputes does not surprise Gulliver, for we are all 'inclined to be more curious and conceited in matters where we have least concern and for which we are least adapted either by study or nature'. Nature has adapted their ears to 'hear the music of the spheres' but they never enjoy 'a minute's peace of mind', living in perpetual dread of the earth's destruction by a comet, or of its falling into the sun, or of the sun's losing its energy (all actual fears of contemporary astronomers). Hence the 'common pleasures' of life are denied to them, and their neglected wives long to escape to the 'diversions of the metropolis', as one court lady succeeded in doing, to 'live in rags, having pawned her clothes to maintain an old deformed footman, who beat her every day'. Gulliver puts this down to 'the caprices of womankind', but Swift, having noted that the Laputans are strangers to 'imagination, fancy and invention', seems on this occasion to find such behaviour very understandable. It is significant that in this third book, with its satire on intellectual deformities, normal human behaviour—which Swift disapproves of elsewhere—is often used as his satiric standard.

Chapter 3

Gulliver gives an elaborate technical account of the island's magnetic system of suspension and propulsion, a parody of scientific papers, and relates their astronomical discoveries. His subsequent account of the political relations between Laputa and the land of Balnibarbi beneath it is more pointed. It describes the methods by which the king can reduce his subjects to obedience, either by depriving them of sun and rain and so 'afflict the inhabitants with death and diseases', or by letting the island drop on their heads. The cities can, however, defend themselves from this fate either by sheltering under natural rocks or by artificial towers strong enough to shatter the bottom of the island. This 'balance of advantage' by which the inhabitants are able to protect 'their liberty or property' was once applied ingeniously by the rebellious people of Lindalino who used magnetic powers of their own to counter those of the island. Whether we interpret the island as monarchy, or as government, or as the colonial power of England, in which case Lindalino's 'proud people' are the people of Dublin, it is clear that all Gulliver's pseudo-science about loadstones and adamant is a Swiftian allegory about the relations between governors and governed.

NOTES AND GLOSSARY:

The revolt of Lindalino: The last five paragraphs allegorise Ireland's campaign against 'Wood's half-pence'. Swift's *Drapier's Letters* are no doubt the 'combustible fuel' which helps to repel Laputa

---

Chapter 4

Through the friendship of a 'great lord at court' Gulliver obtains permission to descend to Balnibarbi, where he stays with Lord Munodi. He finds the people 'generally in rags' and despite signs of labour 'I never knew a soil so unhappily cultivated, houses so ill-contrived and so ruinous, or a people whose countenances and habit expressed so much misery and want'. Munodi himself has an estate which is neat, ordered, and productive, and a noble house 'built according to the best rules of ancient architecture'. But he is generally despised and mistrusted 'for managing his affairs no better' and will soon have to conform to 'modern usage' as devised by the Academy of Projectors. This body of scientific enthusiasts, infected by the impractical spirit of Laputa, is busy devising new rules for all trades and activities, but while it works on its schemes 'the whole country lies miserably waste, the houses in ruins, and the people without food or clothes'.

NOTES AND GLOSSARY:

Poverty: It would be complacent to think that this chapter is wholly about eighteenth-century Ireland, but Gulliver's shock recalls Swift's anger over the Irish poor, who starved while economic 'projectors' wrangled over schemes of reform, of which his own *Modest Proposal* is a savage parody

Lord Munodi: 'Munodi' partly represents Oxford again, but Swift himself also put much energy into maintaining his house and land in model order

Chapter 5

A chapter of sheer high spirits in which Gulliver soberly reports on the projects of the Academy for 'extracting sunbeams out of cucumbers', 'softening marble for pillows and pin-cushions', reforming language by abolishing words, and many other hilarious attempts to reverse the natural order. Some readers cite this chapter as proof of Swift's anti-intellectualism. He certainly based some of his 'projects' on actual scientific proceedings at the Royal Society.

Chapter 6

Not surprisingly, the professors in the 'school of political projectors' appear to be 'wholly out of their senses', indulging in 'wild and impossible schemes'. The opening paragraph is an example of Swift's technique of 'reversal' at its best and it would be unforgivable to explain what happens to the reader who still thinks he can trust Gulliver as a guide. The subsequent project allows Swift to express his opinion of the mental health of senators by an ingenious list of their bodily ills, after which Gulliver offers advice on memorable ways of reminding ministers of their duty. A scheme for ending political factions by brain surgery shows how ironical Swift can be about his own fierce party loyalties. This chapter of hard-hitting political satire concludes with a direct attack on the methods of investigation used in 'the kingdom of Tribnia, by the natives called Langden', where unscrupulous ministers pervert the most innocent letters into proofs of treason. Swift's list of examples is far from innocent. Tribnia and Langden are of course anagrams for Britain and England: Swift is taking his revenge on those who used such evidence against his friends. In this flight of invective he gaily calls Walpole a 'buzzard' and his administration 'a running sore'.

Chapter 7

Gulliver sails from Maldonada to Glubbdubdrib, the Island of Sorcerers, whose governor has the power of calling up the dead to serve him for twenty-four hours, which may be why the palace guards make Gulliver's 'flesh creep with a horror I cannot express'. Of the many heroes of antiquity whom Gulliver is enabled to meet, Brutus is described with the most wholehearted admiration—apparently shared by Caesar. 'I had the honour to have much conversation with Brutus; and was told that his ancestors Junius, Socrates, Epaminondas, Cato the Younger, Sir Thomas More, and himself were perpetually together: a sextumvirate to which all the ages of the world cannot add a seventh.' He sees many others, especially 'destroyers of tyrants', and 'restorers of liberty to oppressed and injured nations', but clearly he does not think that we, his readers, would be much interested in these.

NOTES AND GLOSSARY:

Alexander:	Alexander the Great (356–323BC) expanded Greek power throughout the Mediterranean lands and into Asia. In the battle of Arbela (near the river Tigris) he defeated King Darius III of Persia to win control of Babylon and Persepolis. He died of fever, but there was a legend that he was poisoned
Hannibal:	this great Governor of Carthage (*c*. 247–183BC) led an army of 60,000 across the Alps to attack Rome from the North, in a campaign that lasted fifteen years. The Roman poet Livy suggested that Hannibal used vinegar to soften an Alpine rock-fall.
The sextumvirate:	Swift's choice of heroes may be one of the clearest indications of his own ideals. Understanding what these six men stood for will help you to decide which parts of the *Travels* most nearly express Swift's true beliefs, and whether Lilliput, Brobdingnag or Houyhnhnmland is nearest to Utopia
Lucius Junius Brutus:	first Consul of Rome in 509BC, after expelling the Tarquin rulers. He executed his own sons for treason
Marcus Brutus:	(85–42BC) took his own life when he failed to prevent the restoration of tyranny after he had assassinated Caesar
Marcus Porcius Cato:	(95–46BC) the embodiment of Stoic Roman virtues, Cato helped his friends to escape a siege but took his own life rather than submit to tyranny
Socrates:	(*c*. 470–399BC) was sentenced to death for impiety, but refused to change his opinions
Epaminondas:	(420–362BC), military commander of Thebes, was also relentlessly truthful. He lived hardily and died a heroic death in battle
Sir Thomas More:	(1475–1535), executed by Henry VIII for 'treason', was subsequently canonised

Chapter 8

Next Gulliver calls up Homer and Aristotle, with all their critics and
interpreters who appear ashamed at having 'so horribly misrepresented
the meaning of those authors to posterity'. With this warning to Swift's
critics, including us, Gulliver introduces the poet and philosopher to
two of their commentators. Swift makes Aristotle guilty of a punning
reference to Duns Scotus by asking 'whether the rest of the tribe were
as great dunces'. Next Descartes is summoned to explain his system of
philosophy to Aristotle who expresses Swift's view of all modern theories,
such as Newtonian gravity ('attraction'), as merely 'new fashions'.
Inspecting the ancestry of certain noble families Gulliver finds their
lineages interrupted by 'pages, lackeys, valets' and the like. From this
scurrilous enquiry he passes to a detailed examination of modern history
and discovers 'the secret causes of many great events that have surprised
the world, how a whore can govern the back-stairs, the back-stairs a
council, and the council a senate'. The passage cannot be summarised.
It is an unrelenting attack on every kind of treachery, vice and injustice,
and is clearly intended to describe the normal state of affairs, not the
exception. Few passages in the book are as bleak as this, though the
discovery of 'a barber, an abbot, and two cardinals' in one royal line is
typical of many comic touches.

NOTES AND GLOSSARY:

Homer: (dates unknown, probably about the ninth century
BC) Greek poet of *The Iliad* and *The Odyssey*. The
earliest and most influential of all known poets. He
was traditionally thought to be blind in old age, but
Gulliver remarks on his 'quick and piercing eyes'

Aristotle: (384-322BC) the great philosopher and scientist who
enrolled in Plato's academy when he was seventeen
and whose most famous works—*The Physics, The
Metaphysics, The Ethics, The Poetics, The Rhetoric, The Politics*—dominated these studies for
nearly two thousand years

Didymus: (born 63BC in Alexandria) lived in Rome and wrote
a treatise on Homer

Eustathius: Archibishop of Thessalonica in the twelfth century,
commentator on Homer

Ramus: Petrus Ramus, or Pierre de la Ramée (1515–72),
was a leading opponent of Aristotle's ideas in the
sixteenth century

Scotus:	Duns Scotus (*c.* 1270–1308) wrote chiefly about Aquinas and Aristotle.
Descartes:	René Descartes (1596–1650), philosopher, physicist and mathematician, questioned Aristotle's physics. His theory of vortices attempted to explain the movements of the planets
Gassendi:	Pierre Gassendi (1592–1655) criticised both Aristotle and Descartes
Newton:	Sir Isaac Newton (1642–1727) made revolutionary discoveries in mathematics, optics, and astronomy. He was the co-discoverer of integral and differential calculus, which he called 'fluxions'; he analysed light, using prisms; and his greatest work, the *Principia*, described the mechanics of the solar system. He first calculated the 'attraction' or gravitational pull of the earth on the moon, and went on to describe the law of universal gravitation. Swift's frivolous attitude to Newton is one of his less impressive characteristics
Eliogabalus:	a particularly cruel Emperor of Rome, who reigned from AD 218 to 222, when he was assassinated at the age of eighteen
Agesilaus:	King of Sparta, 397–360BC
Polydore Virgil:	an Italian who lived in England and in 1534 published his *History of England*

'Nec vir fortis, nec femina casta': (*Latin*) neither one brave man nor one chaste woman

Lineages:	to an insider such as Swift it was a simple fact that the Stuart kings, Charles II and James II especially, were governed by their mistresses. Great titles were bestowed on sexual favourites, and cases of doubtful parentage were frequent in some great families of the day
Actium:	Octavius Caesar defeated Antony and Cleopatra at this battle in 31BC

Chapter 9

Gulliver returns to Maldonada and sails to Luggnagg, where he is detained by officials for two weeks until he receives royal permission to visit the king and 'to lick the dust before his footstool', a literal invitation which ensures that petitioners have their mouths too full of dust to speak by the time they reach the throne, and provides a convenient way of poisoning the king's enemies. As his destination is Japan, Gulliver is now travelling as 'a Dutchman'.

NOTES AND GLOSSARY:

The *Amboyna:* this Dutch ship bears the name of a port in the East Indies where a massacre of the British occurred in 1623

Chapter 10

Hearing of a race of immortals known as Struldbrugs, Gulliver amuses his hosts by expressing 'rapture' at this discovery, but his rapture soon turns to horror. The Struldbrugs are not the models of virtue and wisdom he imagines, but 'the most mortifying sight I ever beheld', having 'not only all the follies and infirmities of other old men, but many more which arose from the dreadful prospect of never dying'. This parable has several meanings. It can be read as a sermon, such as Swift might have preached to help people conquer 'the fear of death', or perhaps as a satire on the way people blame their shortcomings on the shortness of life. It is also worth reading carefully as a joke at Gulliver's expense. Compare the final sentence of the chapter, for instance ('avarice is the necessary consequent of old age'), with Gulliver's description at the start of what he would do first if he 'were sure to live for ever'.

Chapter 11

Gulliver assures his readers that this story is unlike anything he has seen 'in any book of travels', which is Swift's way of acknowledging that he got the idea from the well-known classical legend of Tithonus (a prince of Troy who was also granted immortality but denied eternal youth). He takes a ship to Japan and is received by the Emperor (one of the least probable events in the book, but Gulliver tells us nothing about it) who agrees to send him to Nangasac (modern Nagasaki). There he joins a Dutch ship and sails home via Amsterdam. To understand the 'business of the crucifix' one must remember that Nagasaki was the site of a mass martyrdom of Christians who had been converted by Portuguese Jesuits. The Dutch were careful to dissociate themselves from the religion of their rivals. As Swift disapproved of the extent of Dutch religious tolerance he represents them as literally 'trampling on the crucifix' in the interests of commerce.

A Voyage to the Houyhnhnms: Chapter 1

After five months at home Gulliver sails via the West Indies to the South Seas, as Captain of the *Adventure*. This opening account of his first command is full of intriguing clues to his state of mind even before his crew mutinies. After the mutiny he is kept prisoner in his cabin, and then after many weeks set ashore in a strange land. He explores stealthily, expecting to be set upon by savages, and comes across 'several animals'. They sound remarkably human from his description, but 'upon the whole, I never beheld in all my travels so disagreeable an animal, nor one against which I naturally conceived so strong an antipathy'. He is approached by one of these beasts in human shape and hits it with his sword, attracting a crowd of others who climb the trees and pelt him with excrement. Gulliver is saved by the arrival of a horse 'who' inspects him carefully and then consults another horse. They were both perplexed and used 'various gestures, not unlike those of a philosopher, when he would attempt to solve some new and difficult phenomenon'. Gulliver decides they must be magicians in disguise and 'on the strength of this reasoning' makes a polite speech which is very comic in context. From their speech he learns two words, 'Yahoo' and 'Houyhnhnm', and practises saying them with the right accent.

NOTES AND GLOSSARY:

Yahoo: 'Yahoo' has entered the English language as a term of abuse for people who behave contemptibly. Spoken 'in a loud voice, imitating ... the neighing of a horse' it sounds half-way between a contemptuous snort and various derisory expressions like 'Yah!'. English women in many districts call each other's attention by shouting 'Yoo-hoo'

Houyhnhnm: 'Houyhnhnm' is to be said just like a neigh, whether in two syllables as whin-im (like whinny) or in four, who-on-in-im

Chapter 2

Still expecting to meet the human masters of these horses Gulliver is led to a spacious stable, which he describes as a house, and where he is further surprised to see horses engaged in various domestic activities. He is introduced by the gray horse to a 'very comely mare' with her colt and foal, after which they put him next to a Yahoo for purposes of comparison. Now for the first time Gulliver is horrified to recognise

'in this abominable animal a perfect human figure' and he is relieved
that his clothing partly disguises the resemblance from the horses.
Unable to eat either Yahoo-food or the horses' oats he is given a bowl
of milk. 'An old steed, who seemed to be of quality' arrives in a sledge
drawn by four Yahoos, to dine with the family. After making himself
some porridge Gulliver is found a place to sleep, between the house of
the Houyhnhnms and the stable of the Yahoos.

Chapter 3

He sets about learning the language, which is nasal and guttural, 'like
High Dutch or German ... but more graceful and significant'. His
master, astonished to find a Yahoo so teachable, is eager to learn how
he came by his 'appearance of reason'. Throughout their conversation
every explanation Gulliver makes to his master tends to confirm the
theme that men are Yahoos who have learned to 'imitate a rational
creature'. Even to account for his arrival Gulliver has to explain to his
noble master the meanings of mutiny and desertion! The horse is unable
to believe that Yahoos could build a boat of any kind, but as he has no
conception of lying or falsehood he can only accuse Gulliver, in a phrase
the Greek philosopher Plato might have used, of 'saying the thing which
was not'. The Houyhnhnms, like men but more justly, regard themselves
as 'the perfection of nature', but in one respect they are like the other
races Gulliver has met, for his master knew 'it was impossible that there
could be a country beyond the sea'. By the end of the chapter the
Houyhnhnm has detected that but for the 'false covering' with which
he hides his real nature, and his 'affectation' of walking on his hind
legs, Gulliver would be a perfect Yahoo.

NOTES AND GLOSSARY:

Houyhnhnm speech: Gulliver's comparison of horse-speech to German
is a reference to the Emperor Charles V who is
supposed to have said that he would 'address his
God in Spanish, his mistress in Italian, and his
horse in German'

Chapter 4

Gulliver's explanation of his arrival makes his master uneasy, because
such human activities as doubting, disbelief and lying are unknown to
him. To a rational creature the use of speech is to 'make us understand
one another' and to communicate 'facts'. What Gulliver tells him is

incomprehensible. At first Gulliver's description of how horses live in England, with Yahoo servants 'to rub their skins smooth, comb their manes, pick their feet' and so on, confirms his belief that 'whatever share of reason the Yahoos pretend to, the Houyhnhnms are your masters'. But Gulliver next explains the use of spurs and the practice of castration. His embarrassment is matched by the 'noble resentment' of his master at this savage treatment. The Houyhnhnm then comments on the obvious disadvantages of Gulliver's physique compared with the local Yahoos, in an argument similar to that of the scholars of Brob-dingnag. Gulliver makes a third attempt to explain his origins and his arrival, and as this involves explaining the meaning of the various crimes for which his crew had been banished, and 'the terrible effects of lust, intemperance, malice and envy', the explanation takes many days. At last beginning to understand what human nature is capable of, the Houyhnhnm asks for an account of Europe and of England.

Chapter 5

Gulliver explains the causes of war, in two memorable paragraphs which summarise the history of human folly. An account of how these wars are fought leads the Houyhnhnm to his first conclusion 'that instead of reason we were only possessed of some quality fitted to increase our natural vices'. Next Gulliver explains the meaning of law, a strange concept to one who believes that 'nature and reason are sufficient guides for a reasonable animal'. Lawyers, Gulliver explains, are trained from youth to prove 'that white is black, and black is white, according as they are paid'. He gives two vivid instances of how the law works for nobody's benefit but its own, and explains that as English law is based on precedent, to ensure that whatever has been done once 'may legally be done again', the lawyers 'take special care to record all the decisions formerly made against common justice and the general reason of mankind'.

Chapter 6

From his brilliant but savage attack on the law Gulliver turns to an account of the monetary system, by which 'the bulk of our people were forced to live miserably, by labouring every day for small wages to make a few live plentifully'. The cause of this injustice is man's craving for exotic foods and intoxicating liquors and fashionable clothes, which in turn cause 'diseases, folly and vice'. But 'disease' is also a new idea to the Houyhnhnm. An explanation of how men ruin their health leads into a fierce attack on the medical profession which relies partly on the black humour of a list of improbable methods of treating patients, and partly on Gulliver's willingness to slander his own profession. Doctors, he suggests, are quite willing to give a fatal dose, either to please a prince, or simply to make their own gloomy predictions come true. The chapter concludes with an abusive account of Ministers of State and of the degenerate condition of the nobility. No summary could convey the force of these passages, which bring together all the fiercest denunciations of human society made throughout the book and intensify them, without a word to suggest that this is any other than the title of the chapter suggests, a plain account of 'the state of England under Queen Anne'.

Chapter 7

Gulliver explains 'so free a representation' of mankind by saying that his admiration for the virtues of the Houyhnhnms has made him less interested than before in defending the 'honour' of men. Even so, he says, his description was rather biased in favour of his home country. The Houyhnhnm observes that as 'reason alone is sufficient to govern a rational creature' such institutions as government and law are proof that men cannot be rational creatures. They have instead 'a pittance of reason' which they use to increase their corruptions and invent new ones. Gulliver's master now makes a lengthy comparison between men and Yahoos, which at first comes as a relief from the satire of Chapter 6. You probably found Gulliver's criticisms in Chapters 5 and 6 a little extreme. But can you find any part of the Houyhnhnm's description of the Yahoos, from their fondness for 'shining stones' to their sexual behaviour, which is not a perfectly apt parable of human life? If Gulliver is describing extreme cases, and the Houyhnhnm's points remind us of normal behaviour, which is the more effective satire?

NOTES AND GLOSSARY:

Spleen: This ailment of the Yahoos, which was common among the fashionable people of Swift's day, is a mixture of low spirits and hypochondria

Chapter 8

Gulliver sets out to observe the Yahoos, hoping to make more discoveries about human nature. Bathing 'stark naked' he is assaulted by a young female and has to be rescued by his guide. Amusingly he admits that she was not 'altogether so hideous' as the others, and he appears to take some pride in the fact that she 'stood gazing and howling all the time I was putting on my clothes'. His surprise that she was not a red-head, 'which might have been some excuse' for her lust, is one of many personal attacks Swift made on the red-haired Duchess of Somerset, nicknamed 'Carrots', an old enemy of his at the court of Queen Anne. Returning to his account of the Houyhnhnms, with whom he spent three years in all, he remarks on their 'general disposition to all virtues'. They have no 'opinions', one of the causes of war listed in Chapter 5, and no interest in 'conjectures' because real truths carry 'immediate conviction'. Consequently they have neither disputes nor philosophical arguments. Their qualities of 'friendship and benevolence' are universal, so they have no special family affection. They breed only until each couple has two children, though three are allowed in the servant class to provide domestics for noble families. Marriage is not a matter of passion, but 'one of the necessary actions of a rational being'. The Houyhnhnm is shocked by the idea that males and females might be educated differently, 'whereby, as he truly observed, one half of our natives were good for nothing but bringing children into the world; and to trust the care of our children to such useless animals, he said, was yet a greater instance of brutality'. The society is Spartan in its encouragement of physical fitness. Parliament meets for five or six days in every four years to settle unanimously a few items of business such as the fair distribution of oats, cows, Yahoos and children.

Chapter 9

One such assembly is described in this chapter. The council continues its old debate, 'the only debate which ever happened in that country', as to where the Yahoos came from and whether they should be exterminated. Gulliver's master, who has learnt a lot from his visitor, suggests gelding the young Yahoos. Except for a passage on the Houyhnhnm attitude to death, which can be read as a comment on Gulliver's experience with the Struldbrugs, the rest of this chapter is made up of brief comments on a number of topics. More space is given to describing their building methods and other examples of their 'dexterity', than to their history, medicine, astronomy and poetry, which are orally transmitted since they have no writing. Gulliver is clearly more interested in their 'not inconvenient' buildings than in their poetry, though in this Art, with its just similes and moral sentiments, they 'excel all other mortals'. (It is wise to read this chapter bearing in mind Swift's passion for history, his skill as a writer, and his veneration for the 'immortals' of poetry, such as Homer and Shakespeare. But remember that Plato has little use for poets, and excluded them from his Republic.)

Chapter 10

A description of Gulliver's life among the Houyhnhnms, a life of simple needs, simply satisfied, is made to sound all the more attractive in contrast with a seemingly endless list of all the things he was glad to be without—namely people and their follies. His social life consisted of listening humbly to the elevated conversation of his master and his visitors. He comes to loathe even his own reflection and to look on the human race as 'Yahoos in shape and disposition'. A wholehearted convert, Gulliver learns to imitate the Houyhnhnms by trotting like a horse and speaking in their 'voice and manner'. At this point he learns, to his bitter disappointment, that at their last Council the Houyhnhnms had decided that he must leave. His master has reluctantly agreed. How a Houyhnhnm can be reluctant to follow reason is not explained, but perhaps even Houyhnhnms are corruptible. So Gulliver sets about building a boat out of wood and Yahoo-skins—perhaps the most subtle touch of horror in the book. He consoles himself for his banishment by planning to persuade mankind to imitate the Houyhnhnms. As he leaves the country he receives an 'extraordinary mark of distinction': his master raises a hoof for Gulliver to kiss.

Chapter 11

Hoping to find an uninhabited island where he can spend his days meditating on the Houyhnhnms, Gulliver sets a course toward New Holland. He is attacked by 'savages' at his first landfall and then, against his will, taken on board a Portuguese ship. The captain, Don Pedro de Mendez, is probably the kindest and most patient person in the book, and everything Gulliver says about him shows us his warm humanity, yet Gulliver condescends only 'to treat him like an animal which had some little portion of reason'. After a very comical description of Gulliver's stay at Don Pedro's home in Lisbon he is persuaded to return to England and his family. The sight of them fills him with 'hatred, disgust and contempt' and he swoons when embraced by 'that odious animal' his wife. Five years later he is still unable to touch any of his family: instead he spends four hours a day conversing with his horses, 'who understand me tolerably well'.

Chapter 12

To defend the truth of his record of sixteen years of travelling Gulliver quotes some words of Sinon from Virgil's *Aeneid*, to the effect that 'fortune has made him wretched, but has not made him a liar'. Swift knows, if Gulliver has forgotten, that when Sinon says this he has just told an enormous lie concerning the Trojan horse. But Gulliver's next words are true enough. Who, indeed, can read of the virtuous Houyhnhnms 'without being ashamed of his own vices'? He commends the Brobdingnagians as the least corrupted of Yahoos, and then passes to a discussion of the possibility of colonising any of the countries he has visited. Which of his various arguments represent Gulliver's way of thinking, and which Swift's? The whole of this closing sequence, from Gulliver's departure from the Houyhnhnms to his final address to the reader, needs the closest attention. For that reason it is discussed at length later in these notes.

NOTES AND GLOSSARY:

The Trojan Horse: In Book Two of the *Aeneid*, an epic poem by the Roman poet Puthius Vergilius Maro (70–19BC), a select band of Greek warriors hid within a gigantic wooden horse, outside the city of Troy which they have besieged. Sinon pretends to be a deserter from the Greek army, and encourages the Trojans to drag the horse into Troy for good luck. At night the Greeks emerge, and take the city

Part 3

Commentary

The nature of the work

Critical controversy

In the late eighteenth and the nineteenth centuries there grew a legend that *Gulliver's Travels* was the product of a lonely and bitter man, half crazed with anger at a world which had denied him success in Church or in politics, and writing his book as a kind of revenge. To the Victorians especially, with their optimistic view of human perfectibility, their pride in human achievements, and their sentimentalism, the book was comprehensible only if one assumed that Swift was misanthropic to the point of insanity. The novelist Thackeray (1811–63) cautioned his readers against the fourth voyage in particular, which he found 'filthy in word, filthy in thought, furious, raging, obscene'.

Even in our century many readers have found it deeply disturbing. Aldous Huxley's novel *Brave New World* (1932) and George Orwell's *1984* (1949) can both be compared to *Gulliver's Travels* in the way they offer despairing visions of what the human race may come to, yet both writers were shocked by Swift's vision of what man actually is. Huxley found Swift guilty of hatred of mankind, and bases his view on Gulliver's and Swift's obsession with excrement: 'Swift's greatness lies in the intensity, the almost insane violence of that "hatred of the bowels" which is the essence of his misanthropy, and which underlies the whole of his work'. Orwell, whose *1984* imagined a world divided into warring totalitarian blocks in which all liberties have perished, found Swift's concept of liberty disturbing. Despite the fact that 'Laputa' is clearly a *satire* on tyranny, and despite recognising Swift's contempt for absolutist authority, Orwell was disturbed by his feeling that Book 4 is *recommending* a totalitarian state.

These responses reveal something about *Gulliver's Travels*. There have been very few books which have left so many readers feeling that though it is a great book there must have been something wrong with the man who wrote it. His personality troubles them, and what he says about man disgusts or angers them. Could he have read these criticisms Swift might have taken a grim pleasure in such responses, for as he wrote to his friend Pope, while revising the manuscript: 'the chief end

I propose to myself in all my labours is to vex the world rather than divert it' (29 September 1725). And in a later letter he added 'I would *anger* it if I could with safety'.

In fact he seems to have failed with most people in his own day, for the book was a huge success immediately it was published. The first impression sold out in a week, and according to John Gay, who wrote to Swift a fortnight after publication, 'all agree in liking it extremely'. There were exceptions, of course. Lord Bolingbroke, Swift's Tory friend who had turned philosopher, was distressed at Swift's disparagement of human nature, and many felt that to criticise society too generally was to criticise the Creator.

With one kind of reader Gulliver's book has always been a favourite. Children, who generally read a cut version of the first two voyages, have always been captivated by the adventures of Captain Gulliver in Lilliput and Brobdingnag. Swift tells the story with rapid strokes of narrative. There is no tedious psychology to cope with, and the descriptions are enlivened by wonderful comic invention of which the main effect is to convert everyday things into magical ones. Children are invariably pleased by the adventures of Gulliver the gentle giant in the toy-town of Lilliput, or of Gulliver in Brobdingnag, so shrunken that the larks are the size of sheep and a household cat is of dragon proportions. Every child who has held his breath while Gulliver holds an Emperor in his hand, or fights off an invasion of giant wasps, would agree with Dr Arbuthnot that 'Gulliver is a happy man that at his age can write such a merry work'.

Arbuthnot also made an interesting comparison. 'I will make over all my profits to you for the property of *Gulliver's Travels*, which I believe, will have as great a run as John Bunyan.' John Bunyan (1628–88) was the author of *The Pilgrim's Progress* (1678), the popular narrative classic of English protestant religion. Why did Arbuthnot compare *Gulliver* to *The Pilgrim's Progress*? Did he really feel that the books were alike in putting the essentials of a Christian view of life into the form of a vivid story? That it could be read this way is shown by the fact that John Wesley, the great religious reformer, quoted extensively from *Gulliver's Travels*. In *The Doctrine of Original Sin, According to Scripture, Reason and Experience* (1756), Wesley saw Book 4 as a passionate denunciation of war: 'surely all our declamations on the strength of human reason, and the eminence of our virtues, are no more than the cant and jargon of pride and ignorance, so long as there is such a thing as war in the world'. And he goes on: 'Man in general cannot be allowed to be reasonable creatures till they know not war any more'.

This is a vital point. Wesley sees the whole tendency of moral philosophy, religious or secular, to believe in 'the dignity of man' without the grace of God, as 'the cant and jargon of pride and ignorance'. That was precisely Swift's view. Although his book makes no positive religious appeal many readers have seen it as fundamentally an attack on the irreligious concept that Man's reason is self-sufficient, that he can do without God.

One further response is worth looking at. Sarah Churchill, Duchess of Marlborough, whose husband the Duke suffered at Swift's hands more than anyone, was one of the book's earliest readers. According to John Gay the Duchess was 'in raptures' at *Gulliver's Travels*, and it taught her 'that her whole life hath been lost in caressing the worst part of mankind, and treating the best as her foes'. We need not take that too literally, but in her Memoirs she remarked that 'Dean Swift gives the most exact account of kings, ministers, bishops and the courts of justice that is possible to be writ.' Few people were better placed than the Duchess to know exactly what targets Swift had in mind. She could enjoy his clear-sightedness about backstairs intrigues and the malice of courtiers, and his willingness to strike out at corruption, cant and hypocrisy wherever he found it. And while she thought Swift mistaken in his alliances (though she too detested Walpole) she must have admired the courage Swift displayed both in attacking the most powerful men of the age, and in defending his friends more valiantly than they deserved.

So one can see this book in many lights: as the ravings of a lunatic misanthropist, a merry work, an austere religious critique of man, or an 'exact account' of the way things are!

Swift and his intentions

We know enough about Swift to dismiss the first of these views fairly confidently. Swift, in the years he wrote *Gulliver's Travels*, was in full possession of his faculties. He enjoyed the friendship and esteem of the wittiest men in England and Ireland. He was so far from being an embittered recluse that he knew himself to be a national hero, for as we have seen, this book belongs to the decade in which he devoted his skills most fruitfully to the cause of improving the situation of Ireland. He wrote with savage indignation, certainly, but impelled by a passion that is hard to distinguish from the most ardent philanthropy, however abnormal its expression may be.

So it is wise to be on our guard against those who project their contempt for man on to Swift himself. What Swift himself says is ambivalent, as we must expect in a habitual ironist, but it is fairly clear that his anger is reserved for those who mislead, rather than those who are misled. As he wrote in *Some Free Thoughts upon the Present State of Affairs* (1714) 'God hath given the Bulk of Mankind a Capacity to understand Reason when it is fairly offered; and by Reason they would easily be governed, if it were left to their choice'. His work is not an attack on the common man, but on those who, corrupted by their passions or self-interest, misuse their reason to deceive and enslave.

Some of the most illuminating comments on *Gulliver's Travels* are those Swift made himself. His most famous remarks were made in letters to Pope in September and November 1725 when he was completing his book. In the first letter he said:

> when you think of the world give it one lash the more at my request. I have ever hated all nations, professions and communities, and all my love is towards individuals: for instance I hate the tribe of lawyers, but I love councillor such a one, judge such a one ... but principally I hate and detest that animal called man, although I heartily love John, Peter, Thomas, and so forth.

Referring more specifically to his theme he went on:

> I have got materials towards a treatise proving the falsity of that definition *animal rationale* [the definition of man as a rational animal]; and to show it should be only *rationis capax* [capable of reason]. Upon this great foundation of misanthropy (though not Timon's manner) the whole building of my *Travels* is erected; and I will never have peace of mind till all honest men are of my opinion; by consequence you are to embrace it immediately ...

In November, after a burst of anger—'Drown the world, I am not content with despising it, but I would anger it if I could with safety'—He went on:

> I tell you after all that I do not hate mankind; it is *vous autres* who hate them, because you would have them reasonable animals, and are angry for being disappointed.

These are fair observations, though we have to remember that Swift did not always spare individuals.

Some later letters are evidence of the high spirits in which Swift published his book. In November 1726, writing to Pope again, he passes on the story that 'A bishop here said that the book was full of improbable lies, and for his part he hardly believed a word of it'. And in the same month he sent a jesting letter to Henrietta Howard, Countess of Suffolk and his closest friend at court. In this letter he makes several jokes based on his claim that he had never heard of *Gulliver's Travels* and could not understand her allusions to it until he received a copy. Then he rejects her offer to pay for some materials she has asked for:

> the weaver ... has no conception of what you mean by returning money, for he is become a proselyte of the Houyhnhnms, whose great principle (if I rightly remember) is benevolence. And as to myself, I am rightly affronted with such a base proposal that I am determined to complain of you to Her Royal Highness, that you are a mercenary Yahoo fond of shining pebbles. What have I to do with you or your Court further than to show the esteem I have for your person, because you happen to deserve it, and my gratitude to Her Royal Highness, who was pleased a little to distinguish me; which, by the way, is the greatest compliment I ever paid, and may probably be the last. For I am not such a prostitute flatterer as Gulliver; whose chief study is to extenuate the vices and magnify the virtues of mankind, and perpetually dins our ears with praises of his country in the midst of corruptions, and for that reason alone hath found so many readers; and probably will have a pension, which I suppose was his chief design in writing. As for his compliments to the ladies, I can easily forgive him as a natural effect of that devotion which our sex always ought to pay to yours.

Apart from showing that at least one of the Maids of Honour could enjoy court satires, Swift's references in this letter to Gulliver's 'flattery' is a very helpful comment on one of his own satiric techniques.

Clearly Swift did set out to vex the 'world', by which he probably meant the world of politicians in particular, and of leaders of social and intellectual fashion, but equally clearly he knew that his own exuberant sense of humour would be shared by those for whose good opinion he really cared.

Literary models

In some ways *Gulliver's Travels* is a unique work: there is nothing quite like it in world literature. But it shares certain features with many famous works, from serious travel books to comic fiction.

Books of travel are one of mankind's favourite kinds of reading, and imaginative literature often takes this form. Classical epics, such as Homer's *Odyssey*, and the picaresque novel, say, Fielding's *Tom Jones* (1749) and Smollett's *Roderick Random* (1748), which developed in the eighteenth century (after *Gulliver's Travels*), both consist of travel adventures, either fabulous or at least improbable. Lucian's *True*

History, in the second century AD, was probably the first parody of the traveller's tale as such. Lucian (*c.* 117–80) was a sceptical and witty Athenian, of Syrian origin.

The hero of *Robinson Crusoe* (1719), which is an attempt at realist fiction on this theme, shares many of Gulliver's characteristics. Daniel Defoe (1661–1731) based his hero on Alexander Selkirk who had actually been rescued from the island of Juan Fernandez in 1711 by the explorer William Dampier. Swift is engaged in deliberate parody both of Defoe's fiction and of Dampier's accounts of genuine travels. He not only parodies the style of Dampier's records, *A New Voyage round the World* (1697) and *A Voyage to New Holland* (1703–9), but arranges the dates of Gulliver's 'discoveries' of Lilliput, Brobdingnag, Laputa and Houyhnhnmland to coincide with Dampier's presence in the appropriate latitudes. The painstaking way in which Swift mimics the style of such writers in the narrative parts of the *Travels* is illustrated by the storm scene at the start of Book 2, which Swift took word for word from a sailor's publication in 1679. Except that it seems funnier, because more densely packed with nautical jargon, one would scarcely detect any difference from Gulliver's usual manner of narration.

Accounts of travels are also associated with the Utopian genre. The opening of Sir Thomas More's *Utopia* (1516), and that of Cyrano de Bergerac's *Histoire Comique contenant les états et empires de la Lune* (1657), are parodies of similar kind. But *Gulliver's Travels* is both a thorough parody of the travel tale and a book of several competing Utopias. Man's restless search for the perfect society is a perpetual theme of literature, and Plato's *Republic*, More's *Utopia*, Butler's *Erewhon* (1871), Huxley's *Brave New World* and Orwell's *1984* are only the most famous examples of the genre, depicting visions or nightmares of what the world might be. Swift's book gives us four or five to choose from, with the added spice that because of his ironic technique we can never be sure whether we are in a 'utopia' or not.

Finally what we have in *Gulliver's Travels* is an extended analysis of the political and intellectual world of man, an 'anatomy' of society by means of allegory, and an investigation of moral issues by means of many short parables embedded in the book. All the works you will find listed under Allegory or Parable in a dictionary of literary terms have some bearing on this work.

Swift and Utopia

Every so often in *Gulliver's Travels*, amid chapters of innocent narrative, flights of invention, and satirical attacks, we catch a glimpse of something that reminds us of man's perpetual quest for Utopia. Part of the challenge of reading the book is trying to detect which Utopia is the real one. The more ambitious examples of the ideal social structure often turn out to be a satire on man's grandiose dreams: a perfect world is not a possibility for man, and Swift knows it. Some of his more obvious utopian touches, like the various rational schemes for bringing up children, may strike us as coldly repellent, reminiscent of the inhuman economic 'projectors' Swift parodied in *A Modest Proposal*. In the *Travels* it is usually the more moderate proposals that carry most conviction, the appeals to common decency and common sense. The opening paragraph at the school of political projectors, or the modest achievements of the Brobdingnagian state, seem to illustrate a practical ideal for man to aim at.

Indeed the one Swiftian ideal that one can confidently point to was well within the grasp of his age. He believed in a well-ordered hierarchical state. When, in Chapter 7 of the second voyage, he comments on the former struggles between the king, the nobility, and the people of Brobdingnag, he is not criticising the existence of these three classes. A just balance of powers between the one, the few, and the many, was for Swift the natural order of things. It was the duty of every citizen to do what he could to maintain this balance, and to cooperate for the common good. If Swift 'served human liberty' it was not because he was an egalitarian, but because he opposed so courageously any form of absolute power, whether exercised by monarchs or by their ministers. Consequently he despised political factions. Despite his own fiercely partisan activities he believed that he was lending his support to those who stood for common sense and common interests, against Tory Jacobites at one stage of his career, and against the power of Whig financial interests later on. His hatred of war and of standing armies is similarly based. For armies can be made the instruments either of internal tyranny or of imperial conquests, and both tyranny and empire are powerfully criticised in this work. Conservative though he was, there are several issues of this kind where Swift seems to stand in the vanguard of progressive opinion. His views on the education of women, and his attack on the exploitation of the many to enrich the few (Book 4, Chapters 8 and 6) mark him as a radical spirit, ahead of his time. Yet twice in the book he displays a fierce intolerance towards religious dissenters, and his Commonwealth of horses (as Orwell complained) has as rigid a class structure, and as little tolerance of diversity of thought, as the most reactionary of regimes.

Intolerance, however, is a natural quality in a genius devoted to irony, especially in an age which firmly believed that there was such a

thing as normal commonsensical human conduct, and that the task of
the satirist was to scorn all kinds of deviation from that norm (the idea
that diversity of opinion and behaviour are creative and should be
encouraged was a creation of the Romantic age). Swift's 'norm' assumes
that man is capable of rational conduct, that man is quite aware of
what his conduct ought to be. Deviations from good sense and decency,
whether caused by self-seeking, or by following individual convictions
rather than what men have always and everywhere known to be right,
deserve the severest censure. The violence of Swift's attacks on every
kind of intellectual and moral perversion is an expression of his belief
in our common humanity. As he said in a letter to Bolingbroke, 19
December 1719, 'providence, which designed the world should be
governed by many heads, made it a business within the reach of common
understanding'.

Of course *Gulliver's Travels* is so constructed that we do not really
need to share a single one of Swift's beliefs to enjoy his satire. Swift
could be narrow and intolerant, but his genius for corrosive irony and
his pugnacious spirit brought him into conflict with every element of
the 'establishment' of his day. He could pour scorn on his fellow clerics,
the leaders of both parties, fashionable writers and philosophers, and
all the follies of which man—Whig or Tory—is capable. The greatest
quality of the Reverend Dr Swift was surely his irreverence, the one
indispensable trait of an ironist.

Swift's irony

As Swift said in his preface to *The Battle of the Books*: 'Satire is a sort
of glass wherein beholders do generally discover everybody's face but
their own; which is the chief reason . . . that so very few are offended
with it'.

Gulliver's Travels comes as close as any work in English literature
to disproving Swift's ironic comments on the limits of his art. Reading
it is like participating in a game in which the satirist is manipulating
the mirror and the reader is constantly trying to avoid seeing his own
reflection. The moments in which we are 'diverted' by seeing in that
mirror comic or libellous distortions of everyone about us will always
outnumber the fleeting moments of vexation when we catch sight of
ourselves. But Swift is not easy to outwit. He is as agile a player of the
satire game as any man, and this section can only outline some of the
tricks of which he is capable.

We all know that irony means saying one thing while meaning
another. But of course the irony is wasted unless the reader in fact

grasps what is meant as well as what is said. Irony is one of the ways we communicate with each other, either for mutual entertainment, or in jokes at the expense of a third party, or sometimes with genuine hostility. Dramatists use a version of irony in which author and audience are in possession of knowledge which at least one of the characters on stage does not have. In a work of satire written in fictional form, that is, with a plot and a hero, we can expect to find many refinements of both verbal and situational (or dramatic) irony. In *Gulliver's Travels*, where allegory and parable are also employed, the range of possible ironic effects is almost infinite.

Gulliver as an ironic device

Gulliver himself is Swift's most versatile device. His narration is so apparently innocent of malice that our guard is weakened from the outset. His polite and agreeable manner insures us against betrayal, yet he is the cause of most of our confusion. His shortcomings are always involving us in absurdities. The innocent pleasure with which he records that his 'clemency' to the Lilliputians in Chapter 2 was 'represented very much to my advantage at court' identifies us with his ludicrous anxiety to be well thought of in that quarter, just as his surprise at the King of Brobdingnag's 'unnecessary scruple' about gunpowder shows how Swift takes for granted our indifference to human life. Sometimes Swift betrays Gulliver alone for comic effect, sometimes he betrays us through Gulliver. His tendency to make Gulliver give us a superficial view of things, like the political games in the Lilliputian court, accuses the reader of superficial understanding, by exploiting the time-lag, perhaps only a split-second, between reading Gulliver's words and detecting Swift's meaning. At other times Gulliver is liable to defend us so ineptly against some monstrous criticism that his defence only underlines the criticism, for instance when he says in Book 4 that he was unable to prove that human beings are relatively clean since there were no pigs in that country to compare us with!

The author and his mask

The shifting relation between Swift and Gulliver is never quite predictable. In Chapter 3 of Brobdingnag the king clearly speaks for Swift as he contemplates Gulliver: 'and yet, said he, I dare engage, these creatures have their titles and distinctions of honour, they contrive little nests and burrows . . . they love, they fight, they cheat, they betray'. We share Gulliver's blushes at this point. We too resent such contempt:

perhaps more deeply than we regret the vices named by the king. Sometimes Swift exploits his mask in a joke about himself, as he does near the end of the work when Gulliver claims that 'I meddle not the least with any party, but write without passion prejudice or ill-will against any man or number of men whatsoever'. More often Gulliver is made to reverse his moral stance too quickly for us to evade the trap, as in the transition from Chapter 5 to Chapter 6 of Laputa. If you look carefully at this passage you will see that there is in fact a *double* trap. It takes a moment to realise that Gulliver has involved us in a contemptuous rejection of what is most desirable. And it takes a further moment to realise that when these excellent projects are dismissed as 'wild impossible chimeras that never entered before into the heart of man' Swift may well be suggesting that man is so incorrigible that such sensible proposals really *are* too wild to engage our hearts.

Verbal irony

In most of these instances we see Swift exploiting the variable status of his fictional 'author'. But his own favourite verbal ironies are equally various. The use of praise so inflated that we know it to be ironically deflating is a frequent device in Book 1. It is used, for instance, in the opening description of the Emperor, which is composed of every grace and feature that George I certainly did *not* possess, and later in the splendid invocation to that same six-inch Emperor as 'delight and terror of the universe . . . monarch of all monarchs'. A similar use of this technique of reversal is used more seriously in Gulliver's own praise of the virtues of his country throughout Book 2.

More subtle is Swift's habit of leaving something unsaid. What is left out is usually the most important dimension, the moral issue. This can take the form of a report on the Lilliputian debate about how to dispose of Gulliver. Or it can appear in passages like the 4th Book discussion of the causes of war, for instance 'whether the juice of a certain berry be blood or wine'. This way of seeing religious wars is reductive. We know that the issues are misrepresented by taking the symbols of the Christian sacrament at their face value. But the paragraph that follows lists more examples of the causes of wars. These sound equally ridiculous and contemptible, and they *are* contemptible. The technique remains the same, but we have to read the two paragraphs rather differently, and the second makes us reconsider the first.

Such calls on our discrimination are frequently made in another of Swift's favourite games, the catalogue. For instance the list of ways in which men make a living—'begging, robbing, stealing, . . . voting, scribbling, stargazing, poisoning, whoring, canting, libelling, freethinking and the like occupations' (Book 4, Chapter 6)—leaves us to decide whether to discriminate between prostitution, journalism, astronomy, politics, or theft as occupations befitting a rational and virtuous being. It is a consequence of such varied rhetorical techniques that, when at the end of Chapter 6 the King of Brobdingnag makes his judgement on the human race, we are so grateful to return to a plain, direct, style of putting things that we are the more disposed to accept what he says as the plain unvarnished truth.

Situational satire

But Swift's irony is not only a matter of words. The whole conception of the story serves an ironic purpose. How long is it, in Book I, before we realise that Gulliver is not (or not always) an Englishman in a strange land of mannikins but that the mannikins are ourselves and Gulliver the outsider? He is luckily a rather naive outsider or his critique would be more bitter than it is. In Brobdingnag, however, Gulliver remains embarrassingly human. He puts the case for man with all the eloquence at his command, but in a series of innocent rhetorical questions his virtuous host exposes the thorough corruption of our world. No answers are necessary. A pair of perceptive eyes see right through us. That effect is all the more terrifying in the final Book, of course, where Gulliver's attempt to explain man to a creature entirely innocent of what may be meant by opinion, doubt or sickness, let alone wealth, fraud or deceit, puts us all on the rack of situational satire.

Emotional shock

At times Swift finds other ways to embarrass us. Notice how the sexual fantasy of Chapter 5 in Brobdingnag, which plays upon the reader's fascination with the body in close-up, is followed directly by another close-up, of the decapitation of a murderer. Transitions of this kind play cruelly on the reader's weaknesses. The appeal to our longing for immortality is a similar bait in the Strulbrug parable. We are sometimes in a trap that is not merely an ironic game but on the verge of surrealist nightmare, a nightmare which reaches peaks of grotesque imagination in Book 3. Our guide may still be an eighteenth-century gentleman, but so was the 'author' of Swift's *A Tale of a Tub* who made that famous aside, 'Last week I saw a woman flayed, and you will hardly believe how much it altered her person for the worse'. There are few shocks in today's cinema of violence or theatre of cruelty that Swift did not anticipate.

Invective

It is a relief, in a way, to have to deal with one of Swift's/Gulliver's straightforward flights of invective. These range from the description in Book 3 of England as a land of informers, to that onslaught on the legal profession in Book 4. We know, or hope, that not all lawyers are as Gulliver describes them, but we also feel that such savage indignation is fully justified. Swift is protesting, on behalf of humanity, against ills we need not suffer from but for the greed, malice, or indifference, of those who really scorn their fellow men.

Relativity

Unfortunately Swift does not leave us with this rather comfortable enjoyment of seeing our common enemies given a thorough verbal thrashing. There are effects of *Gulliver's Travels* that strike at us all. Consider the structure once again. If the 'nobility' of Lilliputians is contemptible because of their size, or the beauty of a young woman becomes repulsive when magnified to Brobdingnagian proportions, do not these effects leave us with a sense that perhaps all beauty, or value, or dignity, is relative? Is everything we value so meaningless? Is any ground left for our self-esteem? These effects are not wholly negative, though some readers have found them so. Decency remains decency on whatever scale. The problem is to find the few qualities which are not shown to be relative. When we have found those we have found Swift's positives, the firm base from which he launches his ironic missiles.

Major structural ironies: narrative and rhetoric

Reading Books 1 to 3 successfully still leaves us with problems in Book 4. Here all Swift's arts are employed to their best effect. The narrative is brilliantly devised. Gulliver's recognition of himself as Yahoo is so thoroughly convincing that we have to share his despairing admiration of the Houyhnhnms and desire to emulate them. We may feel at the end that we cannot be Houyhnhnms, and would not if we could, and that Gulliver is the victim of a delusion rather than a revelation. But we cannot avoid feeling that our kinship with the Yahoos is inescapable. Man is not the perfection of nature, but an animal with some tincture of reason. For Swift's contemporaries that was an instructive joke. For the nineteenth century it was an obscene libel. But all readers must feel something of Gulliver's identification.

How is this done? It is achieved by the most sustained piece of rhetoric in the book. Chapters 4, 5 and 6 are perhaps the most savage indictment of humanity ever written. It is surely the effect of reading some twenty pages of unrestrained libel on the species that makes us fall so eagerly into the trap Swift has set for us. Chapter 7 is a deceptively calm interlude. Gulliver's master reflects a little on what he has heard, and begins to make a few interesting observations on the Yahoos. There is no malice in this anthropological account, but the effect is profound. Few of us will have taken Gulliver's ferocious account of certain classes of men as a fair account of ourselves: we are not, most of us, ministers, nobles or lawyers. But if Swift allows us to dissent from this savage picture he does so in order that we shall willingly recognise ourselves in what follows. The Houyhnhnm's calm account of the Yahoos is a description, through parables, of the ordinary moral qualities of ordinary men, and we believe every word of it.

A critical commentary

Not everyone approves of the structure of *Gulliver's Travels*. The neat balance between Lilliput and Brobdingnag is not maintained in Books 3 and 4. Book 3 lacks a single imaginative design such as links the opening Books together and returns in the 4th. We know that Book 3 was written last, and it seems to consist of many loose ideas that Swift wanted to squeeze in without spoiling his climax. Yet it does play a role in the development of Gulliver's story and of the thematic development, the satirical argument of the work. To show that development this section reviews the book as a whole, and selects key passages for detailed discussion.

Lilliput

The charm of Gulliver's first voyage needs no further commentary. What is more interesting is how, as adult readers, we are made interested in what Gulliver has to say about this land, and how, as children, we were oblivious of any sense of tedium in reading a political history! And thirdly, what satirical use does Swift make of a relatively simple plot?

The first four paragraphs of Book 1 are a model of economy. For the child reader what matters is that after four paragraphs Gulliver has set sail, and after another three sentences has been shipwrecked. But the adult reader has noticed that the hero is an educated man, a graduate of Cambridge and Leiden, skilled in medicine, mathematics and languages, that he is much travelled. We also notice that he married the second daughter of 'Mr Edmund Bruton, hosier in Newgate Street, with whom I received four hundred pounds'. How remarkably open and frank our narrator is, and how carefully he names three employers and gives four addresses. If he were not so brief he would be a thoroughly tedious pedant. It takes some skill to suggest a dull and cautious man in so few words.

By the end of the fifth paragraph we are in a different world and Gulliver is the prisoner of the Lilliputians. Read that paragraph very closely and you will learn a lot about Gulliver as a man and Swift as a writer. In twenty lines Gulliver reaches Van Diemen's Land, his ship is wrecked and he loses his companions. We know the latitude, the state of the weather, the date, the condition of the crew, and we might be reading a ship's logbook. As Gulliver tells us of his experience he omits no detail, for instance, how much he drank before leaving the ship! He takes scrupulous care to assert nothing that he does not know to be the exact truth. 'We rowed *by my computation* about three leagues'. He 'conjectured' it was eight in the evening. There were no houses or at least he was too weak 'to observe them'. Gulliver is not the man to say 'I slept better than I ever did in my life', rather he must write 'better than ever I remember to have done'. Read the paragraph down to 'I perceived it to be a human creature not six inches high' and observe just how many touches of that kind have convinced us that Gulliver is the soul of honour, incapable of a word of exaggeration or a voluntary departure from the truth in every particular.

The same attention should be given to the gradual introduction of satire, sometimes at Gulliver's expense, sometimes against the Lilliputians. Note how Gulliver, bound by 'slender ligatures' to the ground while he is fed, considers himself 'bound by the laws of hospitality' to these tiny creatures for the 'expense and magnificence' of their welcome. There are many instances of such unconscious humour in his narrative. One of these is the comment on the excellent mathematicians of the Emperor 'who is a renowned patron of learning'. Perhaps their method of building ships in the woods and then transporting them to the sea shows this patron of learning to be a little short of common sense? The reason, of course, is that the Emperor is in this respect the same person as the King of Laputa. Both are intended to remind the alert reader of King George I and his Whig advisers.

Swift has some fun in drawing our attention to the moral significance of changes of scale. Notice what happens in Chapter 3, by when the satire is more insistent. After the entertaining account of political agility, rewarded by coloured ribbons, a report reaches the court that a 'great black substance . . . very oddly shaped . . . and rising up in the middle' has been discovered near the place where Gulliver was found. We laugh at the strange inability of the Lilliputians to recognise a hat just because it is six feet high. But if a simple change of scale can change physical reality, what does it do to moral reality? Have *we* recognised the real moral nastiness of the court we have been shown? Has the informed reader recognised in those ribbons the colours of the noble orders of the Garter, the Thistle and the Bath? Flimnap, a fine leaper and creeper, is mentioned in this connection for a specific reason. For the order of the Bath (the red ribbon) was created by Walpole as a consolation prize for those who had failed to win the Garter. The strange episode of Gulliver's hat is a warning. The rest of this chapter is full of political significance and implied moral comment. We need our eyes open. If they are open what we will see is ourselves.

Political allegory in Lilliput

Behind the charming story of Gulliver's adventures in Lilliput lies a systematic allegory of political events. There are rival interpretations of course, and we need not go into all the details. Broadly, one theory assumes that Gulliver sometimes stands for Swift and sometimes for Oxford and Bolingbroke. The other assumes that Gulliver is consistently representing Oxford/Bolingbroke up to the moment of his flight to Blefuscu.

The first theory is that of Sir Charles Firth who argued* that Lilliput was first written as a Utopia, with Gulliver getting into a few scrapes which should be interpreted autobiographically, and was later revised into an allegory of Whig/Tory politics. So the story of the palace fire which Gulliver extinguishes so improperly is assumed to refer to the Queen's prejudice against Swift himself. Her enmity was encouraged by the Earl of Nottingham, among others, who appears in this book as Bolgolam, Admiral of the Realm, and a man of 'morose and sour complexion'. Nottingham did in fact have a remote connection with naval affairs, and Swift's name for the morose earl, in two earlier ballads, was 'Dismal'. Reldresal, in this autobiographical interpretation, is Lord Carteret, Principal Secretary of State in 1721–4, and a friend of Swift. In 1724 Carteret was made Lord Lieutenant of Ireland and had the unpleasant task of offering a reward for information as to the identity of the author of the *Drapier's Letters*. In Lilliput, Reldresal has to suggest a punishment for Gulliver.

The critic A.E. Case argues that the whole of Book 1 is a consistent

*In 'The Political Significance of *Gulliver's Travels, Proceedings of the British Academy,* London, 1919–20.

allegory of the persecution of Oxford and Bolingbroke by the new Whig ministry after the death of Queen Anne.* So the fire is the War of the Spanish succession, settled by the Tories in illegal negotiations with France. Bolgolam is certainly Nottingham, but identifiable as such by Nottingham's known hostility to Oxford. Reldresal is Viscount Townshend, a Whig who pretended to befriend Bolingbroke and Oxford. Gulliver's flight to Blefuscu is Bolingbroke's flight to France, and so on. Case identifies a whole series of minor characters and asserts the total consistency of the allegory given that Gulliver's experiences combine those of the two Tories, and given that the reigns of Anne and George are combined in Gulliver's tale by making them Emperor and Empress. All commentators agree, incidentally, that Flimnap is Walpole, who by 1726 was effectively Britain's first Prime Minister, but who had been a leading enemy of the Tories as early as 1715, and became head of government in 1720.

So if Chapters 1 and 2 are largely made up of innocent narrative, and Chapter 6 is frequently Utopian, we can see Chapter 3 as a portrait of George's court under Walpole's ministry, Chapter 4 as a general account of England and a history of its factions, Chapter 5 as an allegory of the War of the Spanish Succession, Chapter 7 as referring to the impeachment of the Tory leaders, and Chapter 8 as beginning with Bolingbroke's escape to France.

These allegorical interpretations can be fascinating. You can read Firth's in the present author's casebook on *Gulliver's Travels*, and A.E. Case's argument is in the Penguin anthology (see Part 5). But there are many other detailed interpretations that are almost equally convincing. That Swift's contemporaries could recognise a very precise and ingenious allegory of recent events is true. But what was vivid and meaningful in 1726 remains so in 1978. The story is quite unblemished by baffling allusions. It is a perfect cover-story for Swift's hidden meanings, enjoyable in itself, and capable of illuminating our own time as mercilessly as it did his.

Brobdingnag

Swift seems deliberately to leave us in doubt about the effect of the reverse of scale in Book 2. No doubt we share Gulliver's anxiety when he sees his first Brobdingnagian, even if we remember the groundlessness of the Lilliputians' similar fear in Book 1: 'for as human creatures are observed to be more savage and cruel in proportion to their bulk, what could I expect but to be a morsel in the mouth of the first of these

*In '*Four Essays on Gulliver's Travels*', Princeton University Press, Princeton, 1945.

enormous barbarians . . .' Yet Gulliver does encounter great dangers and suffers at the hands of jealous dwarfs and greedy peasant-farmers.

The change of scale also introduces a note of disgust which did not appear in Book 1. The Brobdingnagians are frequently repulsive, whether Gulliver is describing the nurse in Chapter 1 suckling a baby, or the beggars in Chapter 4. Swift's attack on human vanity is impressive, and because it is increasingly personal it is disturbing. It is the *behaviour* of Lilliputians that makes them, in the end, contemptible. It is the *size* of the nurse's nipple that makes her repulsive. We have to deal with these two images, the nurse and the beggars, very differently. Since we are not in Gulliver's position we would be morally deformed if we saw each other as he sees the nurse. But in the case of the beggars is it not the point that we are morally deformed if we do *not* see them as he does? In the first case Dr Swift has diagnosed a case of vanity: he shows us ourselves in grotesque close-up. In the second he diagnoses a case of moral myopia and he describes the state of the beggars by magnifying their lice and their cancers until our disgust matches his own. Swift was affected by sights of this kind. Most of us have a convenient faculty of not seeing what might disturb us. In *A Tale of a Tub* Swift called it the faculty 'of being well deceived, the serene peaceful state of being a fool among knaves'.

So once again the scale is a moral device. And Swift calls attention to it at the end of Chapter 1 where Gulliver apologises for troubling the 'gentle reader' with particulars about 'discharging the necessities of nature'. They appear insignificant to 'grovelling vulgar minds' he says, but 'will certainly help a philosopher to *enlarge his thoughts and his imagination*'. Nothing is more Swiftian than the joke of placing this clue to his method in the context of one of Gulliver's more absurd, and natural, doings.

Some of the effects of the change of scale are predictable. The humour of Gulliver's feats in Lilliput is matched by the humour of his calamities in Brobdingnag, where the defiler of a Lilliputian palace ends up wading through cow-dung, and the captor of a Blefuscudian fleet is given a boat which can be hung on a nail to dry. Less obvious is the relation between the modes of satire. Where in Lilliput George I is mocked by a flattering description, in Brobdingnag the Maids of Honour, 'excellent ladies for whom I have all manner of respect', are attacked in an account of their morals which relies on polite understatement and assumed innocence to suggest that immorality is only natural in ladies of the court. Politically the method of the book is of course quite different. The events of Lilliput, that is, the whole history of Augustan England, are compressed into a paragraph or so of

Gulliver's first audience with the King, who 'after a hearty fit of laughing, asked me whether I were a Whig or a Tory'. The wisdom of this king, in his cross-examination of Gulliver who now represents the history and the culture of Europe, and his outrage at the idea that he should make use of gunpowder to extend his power at the expense of his people, marks him as one of Swift's portraits of the ideal monarch. Indeed Chapter 7 as a whole is one of Swift's clearest statements of a positive political ideal. The hint at the end of this chapter that Brobdingnag has known its own political disorder makes it all the clearer that the stability and simplicity of the Brobdingnagian state is meant as a model for England to imitate.

In Chapter 6 Gulliver's praise of his country has acquainted us with all its faults. In Chapter 7 his scorn for the defective understanding of his giant host signals Swift's approval. Gulliver is no longer a figure in an allegory: instead he has shrunk morally to a Lilliputian degree of nastiness. By the end of Book 2 Gulliver and Swift have taken up directly contrary positions.

The mood of this book is generally one of good humour, if we except a few obscene libels at the expense of the fair sex. Gulliver's physical frailty is a source of light humour, and his moral myopia is made use of for not-too-savage irony. We are given a picture of a benign monarch and a well-ordered state. And finally there is the comic verve of Gulliver's departure from Brobdingnag and his return to England, very little wiser, but with a greatly inflated sense of his own size.

Laputa, Glubbdubdrib and Luggnagg

People have always argued about the success of the 3rd Book. Made up of several short episodes it lacks the unity of the other voyages. And considered simply as a story there is one important factor missing. Gulliver is not involved, as hero, in events of compelling narrative interest. Children usually like this Book the least, and most critics agree with them. Yet Swift felt that the third voyage was needed to make a transition between the two Utopian books, Brobdingnag and the Houyhnhnms, and Book 3 is in fact carefully linked both to Lilliput and to Brobdingnag in theme, and to Houyhnhnmland through the character of Gulliver.

It is linked to Brobdingnag by an intellectual theme. We remember, as we read of the Laputan astronomers and the projectors of Lagado, one of the most quoted remarks of the King of Brobdingnag, who says in Chapter 7 that 'whoever could make two ears of corn ... grow on a spot of ground where only one grew before, would deserve better of mankind and do more essential service to his country than the whole race of politicians put together'. In Balnibarbi this precept is demonstrated satirically by showing a land where the reverse is happening.

The link with Lilliput is more skilful still, for Swift returns to a detailed political allegory. But where Lilliput tells the story of how Oxford and Bolingbroke fell from power, in Laputa the satire is directed against the state of affairs in the 1720s. The target is the Whig-dominated court of George I. The decay and disintegration of Balni-barbi, the British Isles, under the rule of a remote court and new-fangled Whig policies (as opposed to traditional conservative prudence), is blended with a detailed allegory of Irish resistance to Walpole's policies.

The court of the flying island is easy to identify as that of George I, for King George was a connoisseur of music and his reign was one in which a variety of sciences, notably astronomy, were encouraged. The Prince of Wales also reappears. In Lilliput he had one heel higher than the other because he was inclined to the Tories. In Laputa he is the 'great lord at court, closely related to the King' who befriends Gulliver, and who is sympathetically presented as interested in practical affairs, able to do without a 'flapper', and well-disposed towards Lord Munodi. Munodi, the former Governor of Lagado, is now in disgrace and lives a quiet life on his country estate, the only part of the realm which is properly run. Of course Munodi is a portrait of Swift's friend Oxford, who had retired after surviving the Whigs' attempt to impeach him. Perhaps Swift hoped that in the next reign Oxford would be restored to office. Certainly the allegory can be read this way.

Even Bolingbroke reappears briefly, in Chapter 6, in the passage where 'our brother Tom has just got the piles' is treated as an anagram for 'Resist; a plot is brought home; The tour'. Swift is making a general reference to the belief that Jacobite conspirators corresponded in anagrams, and a specific reference to Bolingbroke who was known in France as Monsieur La Tour.

Once again we can appreciate the general theme of the book without knowing such details. Swift is hitting at what he considered to be abuses of reason. The Laputans are of course comic creations, caricatures of absent-minded professors, so concerned with the movements of comets that they cannot see what is under their noses. But the comedy has its darker side. The erratic progress of their flying island can cause havoc among the people below, and the wild schemes of their disciples at the Academy are sweeping away the solid achievements of tradition and good craftsmanship.

That Swift is attacking the Royal Society is clear: he parodies the style of scientific papers in his account of the magnetic propulsion of Laputa, and many of the lunatic schemes described in Chapter 5 are known to be based on actual scientific papers of the day. But the Academy of Projectors stands for all those institutions which interfere disastrously in matters best left alone. Swift is really stating the classic conservative case, and his Academy also represents the new bureaucratic class—the civil service—which was growing rapidly under Walpole's administration. At the same time he is attacking the new fashion for speculative financial ventures which marked the period. The classic instance is the 'South Sea Bubble', which burst in 1720, ruining many investors, and the reputations of politicians and economists.

Yet the heart of the book is radical enough. The end of Chapter 3 is a thinly disguised warning to Walpole that there is a limit to what the people will endure, and that the penalty for bad government is the overthrow of that government.

The excursions to Glubbdubdrib and to Luggnagg are used to puncture two of mankind's illusions. Gulliver's conversations with great spirits of the past are especially directed against those people in the eighteenth century who liked to think that their age was an improvement on classical antiquity, but anyone who believes in 'progress' is Swift's target here. The other illusion is that a perfect world would be within our grasp if only we were immortal. Thomas Hobbes (1588–1679), the philosopher and author of *Leviathan* (1651) described life as 'nasty, brutish and short'. The parable of the Struldbrugs shows that human beings who lived for ever would only make it nastier, more brutish and eternal. By and large Swift seems to have felt that when the world changes it is usually for the worse.

The third voyage is in some ways the grimmest of the four. The political satire is as severe as anywhere. Despite the high comedy of the Academy of Projectors much of the humour is grotesque, even surrealist. There is an atmosphere of decay and death and dereliction throughout the journey. In the development of the 'plot' this plays an important part. Gulliver returns home armed 'against the fear of death' but with little else to encourage him. When he reappears in Book 4 he is prepared to expect the worst. No wonder he finds in the Houyhnhnms a vision of perfection. And no wonder he leaves his Utopia with such terrible reluctance.

Houyhnhnmland

For his final book Swift has reserved a surprise change of method. Having looked at man from various angles and in various conditions,

Gulliver now finds himself faced with the greatest shock of all. In effect Swift has divided man into his two halves, the intellect and the instincts (leaving the soul to shift for itself), and the instincts appear in human shape while the intellect is embodied in that beautiful quadruped the horse. It is a good choice of shape: even our noses tell us that horses are superior beings!

The theme of the book is of course Reason. Oddly, however, this is the least intellectual of the books, since in a world of reason there can be no disputation (or so we are told). Instead much of the book is taken up with a review of earlier themes. Gulliver explains to his 'master' mankind's methods of settling disputes, War and the Law (Chapter 5), and follows his account of Politicians and the Nobility (Chapter 6) with a fierce critique of the vices of the rich and the parasitical profession of Medicine. Medicine, of course, is Gulliver's own profession, so he convicts himself in Chapter 6. But if the themes are largely unchanged, the treatment is markedly different. In Lilliput Gulliver was the innocent observer of wickedness. In Brobdingnag he was its apologist, called upon to defend humanity. In Glubbdubdrib he makes enquiries about human history and his summary is of course a synopsis of Swift's satirical argument. But in Houyhnhnmland Gulliver is under the spell of truth, and his speech amounts to a shrill and guilt-ridden renunciation of humanity and all its works.

By Chapter 8, of course, Gulliver sees man as a Yahoo. So do the Yahoos. And so do the Houyhnhnms. So the verdict appears to be unanimous. But where does Swift stand, and what are we to think?

There is no single answer to that question, the book is far too skilfully constructed to allow one really to *prove* any line of argument. For instance, are the Houyhnhnms an ideal society or not? Certainly they have the best ordered society in *Gulliver's Travels* (even Brobdingnag has beggars). For this the explanation is simple enough: 'As these noble Houyhnhnms are endowed by nature with a general disposition to all virtues, and have no conceptions or ideas of what is evil in a rational creature, so their grand maxim is to cultivate reason, and to be wholly governed by it. Neither is reason among them a point problematical as with us . . .'

So their perfection is hardly surprising. Their 'cardinal virtues' are friendship and benevolence, which they extend to the whole race. Their life is simple but hardy, recalling the virtues of Sparta more than of Athens in the value they put on 'strength, speed and hardiness'. Because they are guided by reason rather than by appetites their life is without conflict. They face death with Stoic calm. In all these ways the Houyhnhnms embody the kind of virtues represented by Swift's own heroes, that 'sextumvirate to which all the ages of the world cannot add a seventh' (Book 3, Chapter 7).

And yet the reader cannot help feeling that such a life without affection, without humour, without doubt or argument or passion, without any of the circumstances which test our humanity and in fact distinguish the members of that 'sextumvirate' for courage, integrity and stoicism, could have had very little appeal indeed for Swift. How could he have endured those solemn conversations, or those sober poetry recitals? Indeed could he really commend a culture with no books and no history? More important, perhaps, is the thought that the Houyhnhnms are without religion. As a sincere Christian Swift believed in the revealed truths of his religion, truths which cannot be arrived at by reason alone, not because they are unreasonable but because they are *beyond* reason. Reason may be sufficient for a rational creature, but not for a creature with an immortal soul.

This argument can be pressed further, even if the comic aspects of the Houyhnhnms are ignored. How 'rational' is a creature who 'knew that it was impossible that there could be a country beyond the sea' (Chapter 3)? How 'benevolent' is a society which sentences Gulliver (in Chapter 10) to almost certain death? And if this is a realm of perfect reason and perfect justice, how is it that Gulliver's response to his banishment—'I thought it might consist with reason to have been less rigorous'—is almost identical with his response to the sentence passed on him by the Lilliputians in Chapter 7.

Nevertheless we do not have to feel that Houyhnhnm life is perfect to agree with Gulliver in Chapter 12 when he asks 'who can read of the virtues I have mentioned in the glorious Houyhnhnms, without being ashamed of his own vices, when he considers himself as the reasoning, governing animal of his country?'. For the real subject we have to consider is: what is man?

In the Houyhnhnm's view man is a creature who, instead of reason, was only 'possessed of some quality fitted to increase our natural vices' (Chapter 5). He makes the indisputable point, in Chapter 7, that 'reason alone is sufficient to govern a rational creature', and in Chapter 8 the name of Socrates is introduced to support the argument that a reasonable creature would not concern himself with other people's conjectures, especially 'in things where that knowledge, if it were certain, could be of no use'.

But the name of Socrates reminds us that Swift believed that virtue was not a matter of reason but of will, a belief common to philosophy since Aristotle and to the Christian tradition. The horse is perfectly right in his own case. But he is representing a view put forward by Bolingbroke and Shaftesbury in eighteenth-century philosophy, and later on by Godwin, Bentham and the Utilitarians, that reason can make us virtuous. If one is a Houyhnhnm it can. But Swift rejected, with rage and mirth combined, the fallacy that this can be true of man. Man is not a rational creature: reason, therefore, is not enough to govern him. The whole catalogue of human vice and folly throughout this book has one real purpose, which is to persuade us of that.

So is man a Yahoo? The only person in Book 4 who does not think so is, ironically, Gulliver's master. Alone of the Houyhnhnms he is willing to think that Gulliver's share of reason was 'in a degree as far inferior to the Houyhnhnm race as the Yahoos of their country were to me'. Read backwards, that is a clear enough sign of Gulliver's true position, neither Houyhnhnm nor Yahoo, but exactly half-way between them. This is also true of the narrative effect, for by the end of the book Gulliver is thoroughly devoted to the Houyhnhnms, but 'a real Yahoo in every limb and feature'.

The paradox is that we have been brought to face a truth about ourselves by being caught up in a remarkable deception. For in this parable about the nature of man, there are no men to be seen, except Gulliver. And a neighing, trotting Gulliver, who believes he is a Yahoo, looks on his wife and children as Yahoos, yet makes himself a canoe out of Yahoo skins, and appears to have written off the whole human race as unmendable, is hardly the best guide to the meaning of a book which Swift said 'will wonderfully mend the world'.

Of course there is one man in the book, though not in Houyhnhnmland. His name is Don Pedro and he is the closest thing in all Swift's writings to a portrait of honour, courtesy, friendship and generosity. His conduct towards Gulliver, who treats him as a Yahoo, goes beyond anything a Houyhnhnm could understand. For to the Houyhnhnm virtue of benevolence he adds compassion.

Let us pick up the story at the beginning of Chapter 11, just after Gulliver's banishment, and see just how all Swift's skills are deployed in the final pages of the book. From the moment when Gulliver is forcibly rescued by Don Pedro's crew he discredits himself utterly. There is a marvellous consistency in this chapter, but it is the consistency of lunacy. Gulliver, after three years' Houyhnhnm tuition, seems to have lost the ability to draw a rational conclusion from the simplest evidence. Like the animals in Orwell's *Animal Farm* his whole wisdom seems to be expressible in the slogan 'four legs good, two legs bad'. Of course he tells us the truth about his treatment on this voyage, for he could not 'say the thing that is not', but his own churlish behaviour is quite unaffected by the 'great humanity' of the sailors. While Gulliver enjoys the captain's 'excellent wine' he refuses to borrow 'the best suit of clothes he had' since he could not endure wearing 'any thing that had been on the back of a Yahoo'. To Gulliver anything on two legs must be a Yahoo. When he finally reaches home he spurns his family and ends up talking to horses.

But although the 'story' is now over, the satire is not. The final chapter is an exhilarating display of constantly shifting modes of irony. The comic figure whom we left in his stable in Chapter 11 turns to address the reader in Chapter 12, saying that his aim has been 'to inform, and not to amuse thee'. His protestations of truth are comic in themselves, but only a reader who has skipped much of the book will fail to smile when Gulliver claims to have written without 'passion, prejudice or ill-will against any man or number of men whatsoever'. A paragraph later, Gulliver's former self is debating with prudence and pedantry the probable outcome of battle between Houyhnhnms and a European army, but it is Swift who wishes at the end of the passage that men would learn 'the first principles of honour, justice, truth, temperance, public spirit, fortitude, chastity, friendship, benevolence, and fidelity. The *names* of which virtues are still retained among us in most languages . . .' And in the following paragraph, though Gulliver seems to have a few 'scruples' about enlarging his Majesty's dominions by colonisation, Swift suddenly steps in to raise the argument on to a moral plane which is beyond Gulliver's range. It is a Swift we have not heard with such passion before who writes this diatribe against colonial arrogance and butchery, the savagery committed in the name of 'divine right', or the cultural arrogance of 'Christian' conquistadors.

From Swift's moral passion we return to Gulliver, who hopes to reconcile himself to mankind by the absurd remedy of beholding 'my figure often in a glass', and who speaks with unconscious irony, considering how extraordinarily well he recently adapted himself to horse-behaviour, of how difficult it is for a man late in life to change 'old habits'. Next we hear a more tolerant Gulliver who can accept the sight of 'a lawyer, a pickpocket, a colonel, a fool, a lord, a gamester, a politician, a whore-master, a physician, an evidence, a suborner, an attorney, a traitor, or the like' since these are 'all according to the due course of things'. Surely none of us could be quite so tolerant? Certainly not Swift. But Gulliver merges with Swift as the sentence continues: 'but when I behold a lump of deformity and diseases both in body and mind, smitten with *pride*, it immediately breaks all the measures of my patience'. At last Gulliver has discovered the theme of all his experiences, and has hit the nail firmly on the head. The beginning of his last paragraph, too, makes an important Swiftian point, that virtues are as natural to the Houyhnhnms as legs and arms are to us. The unspoken corollary is that appetites are as natural to us as legs and hooves are to them. But Gulliver cannot end on this note of reasonableness. He can share his author's hate but not his humanity, and he falls into the very sin he deplores in his last sentence of all. The very figure of pride himself: 'I here entreat those who have any tincture of this absurd vice, that they will not presume to come in my sight'.

Swift knew that an ironic turn of mind can lead in the end to misanthropy. That is why, at the end of the *Travels*, he subjects his hero to burlesque. Vanity, misanthropy and pride are all compounded in Gulliver's final posture: Swift stands back from this self-portrait, and laughs.

Part 4

Hints for study

THROUGHOUT THESE NOTES, in the summaries and the commentary, you will find questions to pursue as you read the text, and advice on particular passages in the text which it is wise to read with special attentiveness. This section consists of a series of questions and exercises. Some of the questions are answered. Others are followed by notes which you should practise expanding into essay form. And to others you should work out your own answers: you will find some material in earlier sections relating to each of these questions.

Questions

Question 1: *What is the moral effect of Swift's use of scale in Lilliput?*

Book 1 is perhaps the simplest of the travels, yet in addition to the many comments already made on this topic in these notes there is more to be said. In the next two paragraphs I comment on the satirical purpose of Swift's use of scale. You should consider these points, along with the material in the summary and the commentary, and then make a synopsis.

The scale of the Lilliputians is an optical trick, and it calls attention to what we see. It is clear that while matters like the attractiveness of the Lilliputians, and the absurdities of their attempts at dignified behaviour, are noticed by us all as readers, Gulliver as narrator only sees the first. He is also unable to see how ludicrous his own humility looks in this context, or how comic is the pride he takes in the title of 'Nardac', conferred on him. But what does Swift see? Swift, I think, is watching us, as readers, very carefully, to see whether we fall into the moral trap you have fallen into if you agreed with me that Gulliver's humility is comic. Because Swift has carefully devised Books 1 and 2 to make it as hard as possible to remember all the time that morality and decent behaviour are in no way connected with size. Of course we all know that. And we all recognise that when in Book 2 Gulliver assumes that the Brobdingnagians must be barbarians because they are enormous, he is comically wrong. Yet we must all share the feeling, throughout Book 1, that (*a*) these people are comic because they are tiny, (*b*) they ought to 'be good because they are so tiny, and (*c*) their wickedness is especially shocking because they are so tiny. We, of course, being bigger, may be forgiven somewhat bigger sins. At least, that is what Swift expects us to feel.

So this simple idea of little men and big men is really very ingenious. But what is the point of the invention in terms of the *Travels* as a whole? Surely it is to make us realise in the end that while we think we are rational and moral beings we can be thrown into moral confusion by a simple change of scale. A further effect is to show us how easily we become prejudiced, how rapidly we make a moral judgement about a person or a nation and then expect everything we learn about them subsequently to conform to our own preconceptions or first impressions. To test this, read any two or three consecutive pages from Chapter 6 of Book 1 (or Chapter 3 of Book 2, or Chapter 8 of Book 4) and see how many times your opinion of the 'host' people has to change.

So Swift uses scale as one of his techniques of disorientation or betrayal, to show us two things. First, how erratic and variable our moral judgements are. And second, how easily our notions become fixed and prejudiced. Would you agree that both these statements are true, and that they appear to be contradictory?

Question 2: *Discuss the proposition that all four books of* Gulliver's Travels *are unified by Swift's 'treatise' that man is* animal rationis capax *(a creature capable of reason) rather than a rational being.*

Consider what has been said in these notes about the technique of Book 1 and try to decide how much Lilliput contributes to our willingness to share Gulliver's admiration of the Houyhnhnms. Find evidence in the first three books that man is governed not by reason but by habit, prejudice, tribal or national customs, ambition, lust, gluttony, envy, vanity, etc.

Question 3: *How far is* Gulliver's Travels *a book that can be fully appreciated only by a historian of eighteenth-century England?*

You might write out an answer to this question by developing each of the following points into a paragraph:

(*a*) Some historical understanding enables us to see Swift as an author with an intimate knowledge of the political events of his day (see the Introduction to these notes).

(*b*) It is possible to interpret Books 1 and 3 as detailed and systematic political satire (see the 'Political Allegory' section in the Commentary).

(*c*) There is, however, considerable disagreement among scholars about the actual historical meaning of certain episodes. This disagreement is explained by Swift's need to disguise his precise targets so that his book could be published.

(d) Each episode is so written that we can apply Swift's satire to our own experience.*

(e) It is arguable that by concentrating on the historical references we miss the real power of the book as a satire on man in all ages.

(f) The work is so written that it can be enjoyed simultaneously as a story, as moral satire, and as political satire.

Question 4: *Why is* Gulliver's Travels *so popular with children?*

Question 5: *Here is a quotation from Swift's autobiographical 'Verses on the Death of Dr Swift':*

> *Perhaps I may allow the Dean,*
> *Had too much satire in his vein;*
> *And seemed determined not to starve it,*
> *Because no age could more deserve it.*
> *Yet malice never was his aim;*
> *He lashed the vice but spared the name;*
> *No individual could resent,*
> *Where thousands equally were meant;*
> *His satire points at no defect,*
> *But what all mortals may correct; . . .*

Does Swift satirise only 'what all mortals may correct'?

Question 6: *Ask yourself the same question about each of the other couplets in the above verses.*

Question 7: *Was Swift a misanthrope?*

You should consider, on the one hand, evidence of Swift's humour, his charitable activities, his idealism, his involvement in political affairs, and his own statements on misanthropy.

On the other hand *Gulliver's Travels* does appear to criticise man for having natural functions, appetites and anxieties. The satire in some places may strike you as excessively fierce. And you should consider Aldous Huxley's opinion that Swift 'could never forgive man for being a vertebrate mammal as well as an immortal soul'.

Question 8: *How ideal is the Commonwealth of the Houyhnhnms?*

See the commentary on this in Part 4 and be careful to compare Houyhnhnmland with the 'utopian' elements of the other books.

*While I was reading about the project for extracting sunbeams from cucumbers I read that scientists in California were studying the energy content of discarded walnut shells.

Question 9: *How successful is* Gulliver's Travels *considered as a novel?*
This is a complex question, involving several issues. We need to consider
at least three points: the style of the work, whether it has a plot, and
whether it has a hero.

The style of this work is itself a creation of genius. The sign of this
is that we are so rarely conscious of it as we read. The most rapid
strokes of narrative, the descriptions of places and persons, the reported
conversations, are all in the same medium: clear, terse, masculine, free
of elaborate constructions, down-to-earth. It is the style of a man of
plain words and common sense. Yet this style is made the vehicle of
complex effects of irony, and it has to serve two 'authors', Gulliver with
his vision of things as they seem, and Swift with his determination to
show us things as they are. By comparison with Swift's style, almost
any contemporary prose is elaborate and stiff. All the works of the
sixteenth and seventeenth centuries which deal, as this book does, with
politics, history or religion, are written in intricate, decorative style.
Perhaps only Malory's *Morte d'Arthur* (1485), More's *Utopia* in the
English translation of 1551, and Bunyan's *The Pilgrim's Progress*
(1678) could be compared with *Gulliver's Travels*, and these are all
less complex in their content. This work reads like Defoe's *Robinson
Crusoe*, while producing more varied effects. Yet later in the eighteenth
century Dr Johnson's *Rasselas*, Fielding's *Tom Jones*, and Smollett's
Roderick Random all share features of Swift's style. Whole pages of
the last, with its picaresque satire of human folly, could have been lifted
from *Gulliver's Travels*. Clearly Swift's book is in the tradition of
masterly story-telling. But is it a novel, like these works of Defoe,
Fielding and Smollett, with a plot and a hero?

In my view there is a story in *Gulliver's Travels*, and not merely a
record of four voyages. It is the story of a man who undergoes a series
of experiences in a significant order, which in a novel would result either
in the education of that man, or in his downfall. His four journeys are
subtly different, especially in the way they begin and end. His shipwreck
in Lilliput is a mere accident, and he returns home in good company
and comfort. In Brobdingnag his shipmates desert him, and the whole
experience of his stay in that land affects his behaviour for months.
Pirates and a malicious Dutchman abandon him to his fate near Laputa,
and when his disturbing experiences there are over he sails home in a
Dutch ship in continual fear for his life. The mutiny which opens Book
4 is clearly the last straw and his rejection of mankind is psychologically
prepared.

So much for his experiences. What of the man who experiences them?
We are sure enough at the start about our trustworthy narrator. His

qualities of resourcefulness and truthfulness, his general decency and his sense of honour as a gentleman, are in no doubt. But as the work progresses we note some less desirable features: his pride, his anxiety to please, his moral callousness, his patronising attitudes to real superiority. We know from Chapter 2 that he suffers from weak eyes, but it is his moral vision that fails him most often. The closer you look, the more inconsistent he becomes. As the book progresses he is less and less able to distinguish right from wrong. In Laputa he effectively disappears, in that he has no personality left. (In the summaries in Part 2 and the Commentary (Part 3) you will find many illustrations of all these points, and you should look for your own examples).

In the end these characteristics make us doubt his existence as a real character. Although the book looks like a novel its real purpose is satire, and Gulliver is not only not the author of his book, he is not even a character in it, though he sometimes resembles one. Gulliver must be whatever Swift needs him to be at each turn in the satire. Occasionally he must be real enough for us to trust him, but only so that he may mislead us into one of Swift's satirical traps.

In one thing, however, he is consistent. Unlike Swift he lacks the slightest sense of humour, despite attempting a foolish pun on one or two occasions. He lacks any consciousness of irony, as he must if the reader is to do the work of interpretation. A plain blunt fellow at the start, he ends up with very little self-understanding. Of all possible readers Gulliver would be the least able to appreciate the art of Swift, the ironic art of 'saying the thing that is not'.

Question 10: *George Orwell thought Swift a reactionary in politics. Do you agree? What evidence can you find in the book of progressive or conservative opinions? Do these opinions spoil your enjoyment of the book?*

Question 11: *Is* Gulliver's Travels *a book a religious man could have written?*

Question 12: *Some people define irony as 'saying one thing and meaning another'. Does this explain Swift's way of writing? (Read the section on 'Swift's Irony' in Part 3 of these notes, and find one other example of each kind of irony illustrated here).*

Exercises

Exercise 1: *Find two quotations from* Gulliver's Travels *which most accurately represent Swift's views on:*

(*a*) parents and children
(*b*) death
(*c*) science
(*d*) the education of women

(*e*) religious toleration
(*f*) religious ritual
(*g*) hereditary nobility
(*h*) ideal government

Exercise 2: *Memorise three quotations which best represent:*

(*a*) the scale of things in Lilliput (for instance, a woman threading an invisible needle with invisible thread)
(*b*) the scale of things in Brobdingnag
(*c*) the absurdities of the Projectors of Lagado
(*d*) the 'dexterity' of the Houyhnhnms
(*e*) the limitations of Gulliver's reliability as a moral guide

Exercise 3: *Make a list of all Swift's comments on satire in general or on* Gulliver's Travels *in particular.* You will find five in question 5 above, and a number of relevant quotations in the Commentary (Part 3).

Part 5

Suggestions for further reading

The text

The Prose Works of Jonathan Swift, edited by Herbert Davis and others, 14 volumes, Blackwell, Oxford, 1939–68. Volume II (1941) is the standard text of the Travels.
Gulliver's Travels: an Annotated Text with Critical Essays, edited by Robert A. Greenberg, Norton Critical Editions, New York, 1961.
Gulliver's Travels, edited by Peter Dixon and John Chalker, Penguin Books, Harmondsworth, 1967. This edition has an excellent introduction by Michael Foot and good notes.
Gulliver's Travels, with a foreword by Marcus Cunliffe, New American Library (Signet Classic), New York, 1960. This is the modernised spelling edition quoted in these notes.

Other works by the author

It is best to look for *The Drapier's Letters, A Modest Proposal, A Tale of a Tub*, etc., in *The Prose Works*, above, or in one of the many selections in print. A wide selection is contained in the following:
Gulliver's Travels and other Writings, edited by Louis A. Landa, Riverside Editions, Cambridge, Mass., 1960.
A Tale of a Tub and Other Satires, edited by Kathleen Williams, J.M. Dent and Sons, London, 1975

Biography and criticism

DAVIS, HERBERT: *Jonathan Swift: Essays on His Satire and Other Studies*, Oxford University Press, 1964. This contains several good essays but only one on Gulliver.
DONOGHUE, DENIS: *Jonathan Swift: A Critical Introduction*, Cambridge University Press, Cambridge, 1969
EHRENPREIS, IRVIN: *Swift: The Man, The Works and the Age,* vol. I, *Mr Swift and his Contemporaries*, vol. 2, *Dr Swift*, Methuen, London, 1962–7. The standard biography.

JEFFARES, A. NORMAN: *Jonathan Swift,* Writers and their Work, 197, Longman for the British Council, Harlow, Essex, 1976.

QUINTANA, RICARDO: *The Mind and Art of Jonathan Swift*, 2nd edn., Methuen, London, 1953. The major critical study.

QUINTANA, RICARDO: *Swift: An Introduction*, Oxford University Press, 1955 (Oxford Paperback edition, 1962). The best introduction to Swift's life and work.

Critical anthologies

JEFFARES, A. NORMAN (ED.): *Swift: Modern Judgements*, Macmillan, London, 1968. This contains essays on most of Swift's work.

DONOGHUE, DENIS: *Jonathan Swift: A Critical Anthology*, Penguin Books, Harmondsworth, 1971.

GRAVIL, RICHARD (ED.): *Swift: Gulliver's Travels*, Macmillan, London, 1974. A casebook containing essays only on Gulliver.